pathfinder guide

Chilterns *and* Thames Valley

WALKS

Compiled by
Brian Conduit

JARROLD

o|s Ordnance Survey

D0277402

Acknowledgements
I am grateful for the invaluable assistance that I received from the
county councils and various tourist information offices in the
Chilterns and Thames Valley area when writing this book. Some of
their leaflets, plus the high standard of waymarking, made my task
much easier.
For their help with this revised edition, thanks are also due to
Mr I.J. Murray and Mrs C.P. Thwaites who wrote in with useful
information about changes on the ground. I also received invaluable
advice on rights of way from David Coleman and Ian Burgess of
Oxforshire County Council and Sallie Jennings acting on behalf of
Berkshire County Council.

Text:	Brian Conduit
Photography:	Brian Conduit, Jarrold Publishing
Editors:	Thomas Albrighton, Donald Greig
Designers:	Brian Skinner, Doug Whitworth
Mapping:	Heather Pearson, Sandy Sims

Series Consultant:	Brian Conduit

© Jarrold Publishing and Ordnance Survey 1997
Maps © Crown copyright 1997. The mapping in this guide is based
upon Ordnance Survey ® Pathfinder ®, Outdoor Leisure ™,
Explorer ™ and Travelmaster ® mapping.
Ordnance Survey, Pathfinder and Travelmaster are registered trade
marks and Outdoor Leisure and Explorer are trade marks of
Ordnance Survey, the National Mapping Agency of Great Britain.

Jarrold Publishing   ISBN 0-7117-0674-3

While every care has been taken to ensure the accuracy of the route
directions, the publishers cannot accept responsibility for errors or
omissions, or for changes in details given. The countryside is not
static: hedges and fences can be removed, field boundaries can be
altered, footpaths can be rerouted and changes in ownership can
result in the closure or diversion of some concessionary paths. Also,
paths that are easy and pleasant for walking in fine conditions may
become slippery, muddy and difficult in wet weather, while stepping
stones across rivers and streams may become impassable.
    If you find an inaccuracy in either the text or maps, please write
to Jarrold Publishing or Ordnance Survey respectively at one of the
addresses below.

First published 1994
by Jarrold Publishing and Ordnance Survey
Reprinted 1997

Printed in Great Britain
by Jarrold Book Printing, Thetford 2/97

Jarrold Publishing, Whitefriars, Norwich NR3 1TR
Ordnance Survey, Romsey Road, Southampton SO16 4GU

Front cover:	The Thames Valley from Wittenham Clumps
Previous page:	Magna Carta Memorial, Runnymede

Contents

Keymap 4
At-a-glance... walks chart 6
Introduction 8
Walks

1 Wallingford 12

2 Hedgerley and
Burnham Beeches 14

3 Watlington Hill 16

4 Cuckhamsley Hill
and the Ridgeway 18

5 Old Boars Hill 20

6 Dorchester and
Wittenham Clumps 22

7 Widbrook Common
and Cliveden Reach 24

8 Windsor and Eton 26

9 Abingdon and
Sutton Courtenay 29

10 Aston Hill and
Drayton Beauchamp 32

11 Dunstable Downs 34

12 Goring 36

13 Amersham and
Chalfont St Giles 38

14 Cookham, Winter Hill
and Cock Marsh 41

15 Great Hampden and
Little Hampden 44

16 Petersham and
Richmond Park 47

17 Henley-on-Thames
and Hambleden 50

18 Runnymede and
Windsor Great Park 53

19 Northchurch and
Berkhamsted Commons 56

20 Marlow and Hurley 59

21 Aldbury, Ivinghoe
Beacon and Ashridge 62

22 Ibstone, Turville
and Fingest 66

23 Coombe Hill and
Chequers 68

24 Chesham and Little
Missenden 71

25 West Wycombe,
Hughenden and
Bradenham 75

26 Chess Valley 79

27 Lardon Chase,
Moulsford and Streatley 83

28 Princes Risborough
and Chinnor Hill 86

Further Information 90
The National Trust; The Ramblers'
Association; Walkers and the Law;
Countryside Access Charter; Walking
Safety; Useful Organisations;
Ordnance Survey Maps
Index 96

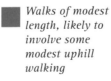

■ Short, easy walks

■ Walks of modest
length, likely to
involve some
modest uphill
walking

■ More challenging
walks which may
be longer and/or
over more rugged
terrain, often with
some stiff climbs

Contents

Keymap

SCALE 1:312 500 or 1 INCH to 5 MILES *1CM to 3.1 KM*

KEYMAP HEIGHTS SHOWN IN FEET

At-a-glance...

Walk	Page	Start	Distance	Time
Abingdon and Sutton Courtenay	29	Abingdon	7 miles (11.3km)	$3^1/2$ hrs
Aldbury, Ivinghoe Beacon and Ashridge	62	Aldbury	7 miles (11.3km)	$3^1/2$ hrs
Amersham and Chalfont St Giles	38	Amersham	$6^1/2$ miles (10.5km)	$3^1/2$ hrs
Aston Hill and Drayton Beauchamp	32	Car park at Aston Hill	$5^1/2$ miles (8.9km)	$2^1/2$ hrs
Chesham and Little Missenden	71	Chesham	9 miles (14.5km)	$4^1/2$ hrs
Chess Valley	79	Between Little Chalfont and Latimer	$9^1/2$ miles (15.3km)	5 hrs
Cookham, Winter Hill and Cock Marsh	41	Car park at Cookham Moor, near Cookham	$6^1/2$ miles (10.5km)	$3^1/2$ hrs
Coombe Hill and Chequers	68	Wendover	8 miles (12.9km)	$4^1/2$ hrs
Cuckhamsley Hill and the Ridgeway	18	Cuckhamsley Hill	4 miles (6.4km)	2 hrs
Dorchester and Wittenham Clumps	22	Dorchester	$4^1/2$ miles (7.2km)	2 hrs
Dunstable Downs	34	Robertson Corner (visitor centre)	$4^1/2$ miles (7.2km)	$2^1/2$ hrs
Goring	36	Goring	6 miles (9.5km)	3 hrs
Great Hampden and Little Hampden	44	Cockshoots Wood car park	$6^1/2$ miles (10.5km)	3 hrs
Hedgerley and Burnham Beeches	14	Burnham Beeches	$3^1/2$ miles (5.5km)	$1^1/2$ hrs
Henley-on-Thames and Hambleden	50	Henley-on-Thames	7 miles (11.3km)	$3^1/2$ hrs
Ibstone, Turville and Fingest	66	Ibstone Common	8 miles (12.9km)	4 hrs
Lardon Chase, Moulsford and Streatley	83	Car park at Lardon Chase	10 miles (16km)	5 hrs
Marlow and Hurley	59	Marlow	7 miles (11.3km)	$3^1/2$ hrs
Northchurch and Berkhamsted Commons	56	Berkhamsted	7 miles (11.3km)	$3^1/2$ hrs
Old Boars Hill	20	Wootton	5 miles (8km)	$2^1/2$ hrs
Petersham and Richmond Park	47	Richmond	$6^1/2$ miles (10.5km)	$3^1/2$ hrs
Princes Risborough and Chinnor Hill	86	Princes Risborough	$10^1/2$ miles (16.7km)	$5^1/2$ hrs
Runnymede and Windsor Great Park	53	Bishopsgate entrance, Windsor Great Park	7 miles (11.3km)	$3^1/2$ hrs
Wallingford	12	Wallingford	3 miles (4.8km)	$1^1/2$ hrs
Watlington Hill	16	Car park at Watlington Hill	$3^1/2$ miles (5.5km)	2 hrs
West Wycombe, Hughenden and Bradenham	75	West Wycombe	$8^1/2$ miles (13.5km)	$4^1/2$ hrs
Widbrook Common and Cliveden Reach	24	Boulter's Lock, just north of Maidenhead	$5^1/2$ miles (8.9km)	$2^1/2$ hrs
Windsor and Eton	26	Windsor	$5^1/2$ miles (8.9km)	$2^1/2$ hrs

Comments

There are two attractive villages, the fine town of Abingdon and lengthy, enjoyable stretches of walking beside the Thames.

This route combines superb views from the Chilterns escarpment with some highly enjoyable walking through the beautiful and extensive woodlands of the Ashridge Estate.

The outward route between Amersham and Chalfont St Giles is above the delightful Misboune Valley; the return leg takes you along the valley bottom.

This walk provides a contrast between the wooded slopes of Aston Hill above the Vale of Ayulesbury, and towpath walking beside an arm of the Grand Union Canal.

You walk through a rolling landscape of well-wooded dry valleys and about halfway round pass one of the most interesting churches in the Chilterns.

This lengthy walk covers woodland, including part of the outstanding Chipperfield Common, and riverside, linking four villages in the attractive Chess valley. Parts of the walk may be muddy.

After climbing to a grand viewpoint above the Thames, the route descends to the river and follows it around a long bend. A pleasant walk with only gentle climbs and fine views over the Thames valley.

A classic walk that includes one of the most magnificent viewpoints on the Chiltern escarpment, some splendid wooded stretches and a view of Chequers.

This walk takes you across part of the open and largely empty chalk downs that lie to the west of the Thames Valley – a stark contrast with the wooded Chilterns.

There are grand views over the Thames Valley from Wittenham Clumps, plus attractive riverside meadows and a fine medieval abbey to visit.

After passing by the unusual Whipsnade 'Tree Cathedal' the route concludes with a magnificent walk along the crest of the Dunstable Downs.

There is plenty of attractive woodland walking and towards the end grand views across the Thames Valley to the Berkshire Downs.

The walk takes you through a surprisingly remote Chilterns landscape, passing by the churches at Great Hampden and Little Hampden.

Much of the route of this walk is through the splendid woodlands of Burnham Beeches, a delight at any time of the year.

This walk links a well-known riverside town and an attractive Chilterns village. There are fine views and the last part hugs the banks of the Thames.

The walk takes you through a typical Chilterns landscape and includes two attractive vilages with fine medieval churches.

A walk across the open expanses of the Berkshire Downs is followed by a delightful stretch beside the Thames. At the end, you climb to a superb viewpoint above the river.

There are fine views across the valley and some splendid riverside walking beside the Thames between Hurley and Marlow.

After an initial stretch by a canal towpath, the remainder of the route is across the well-wooded commons that lie to the north of Berkhamsted.

A pleasant walk through the attractive rural surroundings of Oxford. The highlight is the memorable view of the city, with its famous 'dreaming spires', from Old Boars Hill.

After an initial stroll by the Thames, the route climbs on to a ridge above the river and follows it through the remarkably open and unspoilt expanses of Richmond Park.

This walk is through a Chilterns landscape at its finest. It includes three villages, a pleasant town and a magnificent view from the escarpment at Chinnor Hill.

Plenty of variety and historic interest on this walk that includes the riverside meadows where Magna Carta was signed, part of Windsor Great Park and distant views of the great castle.

Pleasant walking by the Thames and the chance to explore an interesting old town are the chief ingredients of this short and easy walk.

The summit of Watlington Hill provides extensive views across the Oxford Plain and is the starting point for this short but highly enjoyable walk.

Between the three great country houses passed on this walk, there are some grand stretches of woodland and superb views over the Chilterns from a ridge-top path.

The first half of the route to Cookham is mostly across meadows and marshland; the second half is along Cliveden Reach, one of the finest stretches of the Thames.

Striking views of Windsor Castle from the banks of the Thames are enjoyed on the latter stages of this walk. The route also takes in the playing-fields of Eton and views of the College.

At-a-glance...

Introduction to the Chilterns and the Thames Valley

The Chilterns form part of the long line of chalk hills stretching intermittently across southern and eastern England, in a roughly north-east to northerly direction from Wiltshire to the Yorkshire coast. They are both the highest and most distinctive part of that chain, extending from the Thames Valley across Oxfordshire, Buckinghamshire, Hertfordshire and Bedfordshire, before petering out in the flatter country around Luton. To the south and west they are bordered by the Thames, on the other side of which the chalk hills continue as the Berkshire Downs. The chief contrast between the Berkshire Downs and the Chilterns is that the former mainly comprise open, rolling expanses, whereas the latter are far more wooded. The Chilterns, however, do become more open in their most easterly stretches in the area of the Dunstable Downs.

There are some obvious similarities between the Chilterns and the Cotswolds, their limestone counterparts some 40 miles (64km) to the west. Both ranges are partially bordered by the Thames, both are aligned on a roughly south-west/north-east axis, both have a steep western escarpment, and conversely in both cases their rivers mainly drain south-eastwards, flowing through a series of gentle valleys and eventually into the Thames.

Punctuating the western escarpment of the Chilterns is a succession of fine viewpoints – Watlington Hill, Chinnor Hill, Ivinghoe Beacon and Dunstable Downs – overlooking the clay lowlands of the Oxford Plain, Vale of Aylesbury and Bedfordshire. The highest of these is Coombe Hill (852ft/260m), a magnificent vantage point owned and preserved by the National Trust and crowned by a monument to the Boer War.

Because of its combination of scenery and solitude, allied with easy access to London, this area has long been popular with political leaders and other eminent figures. Chequers, visible from Coombe Hill, has been the official country residence of British prime ministers since it was given to the nation for that purpose in 1917. Benjamin Disraeli lived at Hughenden Manor near High Wycombe and is buried in the churchyard there. Herbert Asquith and the writer George Orwell are buried at Sutton Courtenay near Abingdon and W.H. Smith, founder of the books and stationery empire, is buried at Hambleden. The 19th-century Prime Minister Lord John Russell is buried in the Russell family vault in the church at Chenies in the Chess valley, and Clement Attlee lived at Prestwood near Great Missenden.

Many would claim that the chief glory of the Chilterns are the beech woods that extend over much of the area, and indeed it is these that gave rise to the traditional furniture industry of High Wycombe, Chesham and other towns in the area. Walking through these woods is always sheer delight, but inevitably they look best when clothed in autumnal tints of brown and gold. The frequent arrows painted on tree trunks to indicate the line of the many public footpaths that thread their way through these woods are invaluable and make for generally trouble-free walking.

The Thames at Goring Lock

Another attractive feature of the Chilterns is their many dry valleys, which also provide pleasant walking. In fact rivers are something of a rarity and are generally little more than streams. Two exceptions are the rivers Misbourne and Chess, which both flow through attractive valleys. Cultivated farmland, managed woodland, small manor houses, picturesque villages, pleasant market towns and imposing stately homes have been added to this natural beauty over the centuries to create a neat, orderly landscape, doubly valuable for being so near London.

South of the Chilterns the Thames flows through a broad, undulating valley, bordered by Oxfordshire, Berkshire and Buckinghamshire, before continuing through London and on to its estuary. This is a different terrain and a different kind of walking. For most of the river's length public footpaths line at least one bank – in some areas both banks – at times crossing flat meadows with wide vistas and at other times proceeding either through or below fine wooded stretches. A series of historic towns and delightful riverside villages add to the pleasures of walking by the Thames, and a succession of viewpoints above the valley – Wittenham Clumps, Winter Hill, Cooper's Hill and Richmond Hill – give superb views over the winding river. Perhaps the most spectacular views are those on either side of the Goring Gap, where the valley narrows as the Thames cuts through the gap between the Chilterns and the Berkshire Downs.

Throughout the centuries proximity to London has ensured that this area has always been in the mainstream of English history and has played a vital role in the nation's communications network. Probably the oldest routeway in the country, known as the Ridgeway to the west of the Thames and the Icknield Way to the east, follows the line of the chalk ridge across the region, part of a prehistoric trackway from Dorset to Norfolk. Much of this route now enjoys a new lease of life as the Ridgeway National Trail.

The Thames itself has always been one of the chief arteries of English history and many important events have taken place near its banks.

Windsor Castle, the oldest continuous royal residence and main centre of royal power for over nine centuries, rises majestically above it. On the opposite bank stands Eton, the country's most prestigious public school and upstream is Oxford, England's oldest university. A few miles downstream, on Runnymede Meadows, King John was forced to sign Magna Carta in 1215, and a little further downstream is Hampton Court Palace, the nearest England has to a Versailles. Beyond that are the fragmentary remains of Richmond Palace, built by the founder of the Tudor dynasty Henry VII, and where that same dynasty came to an end with the death of Elizabeth I in 1603.

The towns that line the Thames mainly grew up at important bridging points. Despite increased traffic, suburban expansion and the establishment of new hi-tech industries around their fringes, most of them have managed to preserve their individuality and attractive qualities. Abingdon and Wallingford are two good examples. Although they have both lost their major outstanding medieval buildings – only fragments survive of Abingdon Abbey and Wallingford Castle – they still retain a historic 'feel' and possess some fine old buildings, as well as impressive bridges and attractive riverside locations. Marlow and Henley grew up later, as fashionable Georgian and Victorian riverside resorts and desirable residential towns, and much of their genteel atmosphere survives. Dorchester, standing near the confluence of the Thames and Thame, was once the major ecclesiastical centre of the region. Now it is a sleepy but appealing backwater, with only part of the church surviving from its large medieval abbey. Windsor of course still retains its greatest asset, the magnificent royal castle, containing buildings from the 11th to the 19th centuries, the major tourist attraction of the region.

Whereas the principal towns of the Thames Valley grew up at crossing-points over the river, the main Chiltern towns – High Wycombe, Princes Risborough, Amersham and Berkhamsted – were established at strategic gaps in the hills which became major routeways between London and the midlands and north of England. Early roads and tracks through these gaps were successively upgraded and added to over the centuries. The 18th century produced canals, the 19th and early 20th centuries brought the railways, and the most recent developments are the

Typical Chilterns landscape near Bledlow

Introduction

motorways. Berkhamsted is a particularly interesting town in which to observe these changes; here the remains of the 11th-century Norman castle (itself a recognition of the strategic importance of the site) overlook the A41, the Grand Union Canal and main railway line from London to the midlands, north-west and Scotland.

One quality of the region that is likely to make itself quickly apparent to any walker is that despite the main roads, motorways and railways, despite the proximity of Heathrow airport and the seemingly inexorable spread of suburban London, many parts still manage to preserve an air of peace and tranquillity that gives the impression that they are genuinely off the beaten track. This is more true of the Chilterns than the Thames Valley; in the latter area there always appears to be plenty of activity and traffic, albeit of the leisure variety, on the river. But in areas of the Chilterns there are a number of delightful and largely unchanged villages – like Hambleden, Turville, Fingest, Bradenham, Bledlow, Sarratt and Aldbury – and lonely valleys and silent beech woods that could be both remote in distance from London and far in time from the 20th century.

'Civilised' is perhaps an appropriate adjective to describe walking in the Chilterns and Thames Valley. The landscape is pleasant and gentle rather than dramatic, intimate rather than challenging, a landscape of rolling wooded hills and arable fields, open commons and sheltered valleys, largely tamed over the centuries. Given the obvious commercial, transport and population pressures in this part of England, it is a landscape that has survived remarkably intact and unspoilt. Even within the boundaries of the capital itself, a satisfyingly long rural walk can be taken in Richmond Park, and the view over the Thames from Richmond Hill still looks much as it did when painted 200 years ago by Turner.

There is plenty of varied walking in the area, with mainly flat or gently undulating rambles by the Thames contrasting with more energetic walks in the hills. Waymarking is of a high standard, among the best in the country, and although some muddy and overgrown stretches of path can be found in the remoter and less frequently walked areas, paths, stiles and footbridges are generally in a good condition. Much of the credit for this must go to the active and ever-watchful Chiltern Society. Two national trails, the Ridgeway and the Thames Path, pass through the area and most of the county councils in the region have devised short- and middle-distance routes and circular walks which, like the national trails, benefit from good waymarking.

Put on your boots and rucksack, pick up a map or guidebook and you will realise that in this highly vulnerable area of the Home Counties, you can still quickly escape into a world of peace and solitude, of quiet and unspoilt country, that perhaps you felt was only attainable in the more remote and sparsely populated parts of England. Long may this state of affairs continue.

SUN 14.3.99

Wallingford

Start	Wallingford, on east side of bridge
Distance	3 miles (4.8km)
Approximate time	1½ hours
Parking	Wallingford
Refreshments	Pubs and cafés at Wallingford
Ordnance Survey maps	Landranger 175 (Reading & Windsor), Explorer 3 (Chiltern Hills South)

Attractive riverside scenery and the chance to explore the interesting old town of Wallingford are the main features of this easy walk along field and woodland paths, finishing with a pleasant half-mile (800m) stroll by the banks of the Thames.

Wallingford is an ancient town and one of the few in England that still possesses its Saxon earth defences. These were constructed around three sides of the town; the fourth side was protected by the Thames. Of the castle – built in the late 11th century by William the Conqueror to guard this important river crossing, and one of the largest in the country – only a few crumbling walls remain, but the site is an attractive one, now a public park, with fine views over the Thames Valley. Despite being destroyed by the Danes in 1006, decimated by the Black Death in 1349 and

Wallingford

SCALE 1:25000 or 2½ INCHES to 1 MILE 4CM to 1KM

0	200	400	600	800 METRES	1
					KILOMETRES
					MILES
0	200	400	600 YARDS	½	

devastated by fire in 1675, Wallingford retains an air of antiquity. Its surviving churches, a 17th-century town hall and some fine Georgian houses, along with the Saxon ramparts and Norman castle site, all testify to its former greatness.

From the car park turn left to head up to the road, continue along it for 50 yds (46m) and just before the entrance to a camp and caravan site, turn right along a tree-lined track **Ⓐ**. At a fork just in front of a metal gate take the left-hand tree-lined path, which later emerges into more open country and continues across fields between wire fences.

At a T-junction turn right along a concrete track and then turn sharp left over a stile to follow a path straight across a field. Bear slightly right at the far end to continue across the next field, climb a stile and turn left along a track below an embankment up to a road. Turn right to a roundabout, cross over and almost immediately turn right over a stile **Ⓑ** to

join the Ridgeway. Walk along a tree-lined path, cross a track, climb a stile and continue through woodland. Later the path passes through a gap in the fence on the right, continuing alongside a road to reach a junction of paths just to the left of a new footpath underpass **Ⓒ**.

Turn right, pass under the road and continue along a paved path. Where this bears right through a gate, keep ahead along a tree-lined path, passing to the left of school buildings. On reaching a farm, climb a stile to the left of a house and continue along a track, between farm buildings on the left and a house on the right. Climb another stile and keep ahead along the right-hand edge of a meadow by a wire fence on the right.

After about 50 yds (46m) turn left by a waymarked post and head straight across the meadow – there is no visible path – to the river. Turn right and follow the Thames back to Wallingford Bridge, enjoying attractive views of the houses of Wallingford on the opposite bank. Pass under the bridge and turn right to return to the car park. ●

Hedgerley and Burnham Beeches (side running title)

Hedgerley and Burnham Beeches

Start	Burnham Beeches, on corner of A355 and Harehatch Lane one mile (1.6km) north of Farnham Common
Distance	3½ miles (5.6km)
Approximate time	1½ hours
Parking	Small parking area on corner of A355 and Harehatch Lane. Alternatively, roadside parking at Hedgerley Hill just south of Ⓑ
Refreshments	Pubs at Hedgerley
Ordnance Survey maps	Landranger 175 (Reading & Windsor), Explorer 3 (Chiltern Hills South)

Burnham Beeches, a large expanse of natural and unspoilt woodland lying between Beaconsfield and Slough, was bought by the Corporation of the City of London in 1879 to be preserved for public enjoyment and recreation. It is renowned for its many gnarled, ancient trees. After heading across farmland and along a lane to the village of Hedgerley, the walk continues mostly through the northern part of this attractive and popular area. Almost the whole route is well waymarked with Buckinghamshire County Council 'Circular Walk' signs.

Begin by crossing the A355 and taking the tarmac drive opposite to Pennlands Farm. Follow the drive – mostly tree-lined – down to the farm, pass to the right of it and continue along the track ahead, between a wire fence on the left and a hedge on the right, to go through a gate on to a lane.

Keep straight ahead along narrow Kiln Lane, passing in front of a row of cottages, for just under ½ mile (800m) to a T-junction in the pleasant and secluded village of Hedgerley Ⓐ. The main part of the village and the rebuilt 19th-century church are to the left, but the route continues to the right along a road for ¼ mile (400m), heading uphill between trees. After passing Gregory Road on the

right turn right Ⓑ, at a half-hidden public footpath sign, along a tarmac path between garden fences and hedges.

If parking at Hedgerley Hill a little further on along the road, you join the walk at this public footpath sign.

Cross a road and continue along the path opposite, also between fences, passing through a wooden barrier to a junction of paths on the edge of woodland. Keep ahead, in the direction of a Circular Walk waymarked post, along a woodland path; at a fork ahead continue along the left-hand path. At another fork follow the direction of a waymark to take the left-hand path again and follow the regular waymarks through the wood to climb a stile and continue to a road. Turn right, keep ahead at a crossroads and, ¼ mile (400m) further on, turn left  over a stile into woodland. Walk through the wood, by a fence on the left, and climb a stile on to the A355 again. Cross the road, climb a stile opposite and continue along a path between fences through a lovely area of woodland to climb another stile on to a lane **D**.

Cross the lane, go through a white gate to enter Burnham Beeches and walk along a concrete drive. Pass in front of houses and continue along the path ahead through Egypt Woods, the northern part of Burnham Beeches and named after a former gypsy encampment. The path heads downhill to a fork at the bottom. Here take the left-hand path – the waymarked post is almost obscured by bracken – to continue gently uphill to a

In Egypt Woods, Burnham Beeches

T-junction of paths on the edge of woodland **E**. At this point follow the Circular Walk sign sharply to the right along a path that keeps along the left-hand edge of woodland, by a wire fence on the left, then continues once more through the trees.

Follow this well-waymarked path for ½ mile (800m), eventually climbing a stile and keeping ahead to go over another one on to the lane at the starting point. ●

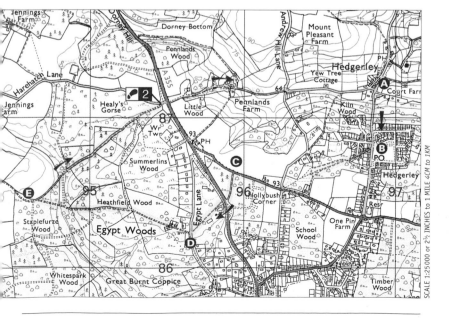

Watlington Hill

Start	National Trust car park at Watlington Hill
Distance	3½ miles (5.6km)
Approximate time	2 hours
Parking	Watlington Hill
Refreshments	None
Ordnance Survey maps	Landranger 175 (Reading & Windsor), Explorer 3 (Chiltern Hills South)

From the top of Watlington Hill, one of the high points on the Chiltern escarpment and a superb viewpoint overlooking the clay lowlands of the Oxford Plain, this walk descends to the base of the hill to follow a short section of the Ridgeway. An easy ascent enables you to regain the top of the escarpment at Christmas Common and return to the start.

Begin by taking the downhill track that leads off from the far end of the car park to walk below a superb canopy of beeches. Go through a kissing-gate and bear slightly right, in the direction of a white arrow on a tree trunk, to continue gently downhill. This attractive path sometimes winds between trees and at other times keeps along the left edge of woodland, with fine open views over the valley on the left. Go over a stile, continue, climb

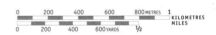

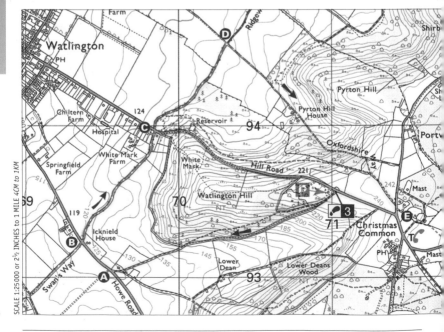

two more stiles in quick succession and keep ahead to reach a track. Turn right along it to the B480 and turn right **A** along the road (there are no verges).

After ¼ mile (400m), opposite a sign to Lys Mill, turn right **B** on to an enclosed track to join the Ridgeway. Follow the track to a road **C**, cross the road and continue along the broad track opposite as far as a crossroads of tracks **D**. Here turn right along a wide, rough tarmac track to join the Oxfordshire Way. Pyrton Hill is the prominent wooded hill to the left and Watlington Hill is to the right.

An initial, almost imperceptible ascent to Pyrton Hill House is followed by a steeper climb along what has now become a much narrower path. The path curves slightly left to enter woodland. Near the

Watlington Hill

top, look out for a stile and an Oxfordshire Way sign on the right. Climb the stile – ahead you can see the radio mast on Christmas Common – walk across the corner of a field and bear left to keep along the edge of the field, by a wire fence and line of trees on the right, to a stile. Climb it and continue, soon climbing another stile to emerge on to the road at Christmas Common.

Turn right, then turn right again at a junction ahead **E**, in the Watlington direction, and follow the road for ¼ mile (400m) back to the car park. Just before turning into the car park, pause to admire the grand view ahead from the top of the escarpment over the Oxford Plain. ●

Cuckhamsley Hill and the Ridgeway

Start	Cuckhamsley Hill, at end of lane 2½ miles (4km) south of East Hendred
Distance	4 miles (6.4km)
Approximate time	2 hours
Parking	Cuckhamsley Hill
Refreshments	None
Ordnance Survey maps	Landranger 174 (Newbury & Wantage), Pathfinder 1155, SU48/58 (Wantage (East) & Didcot (South))

Crossed by the Ridgeway, Cuckhamsley Hill rises to a height of 756ft (230m) above the downs near the border between Oxfordshire and Berkshire. This short walk explores an area of remote, virtually uninhabited countryside characterised by wide and sweeping vistas; the openness of the downs here to the west of the Thames Valley is in striking contrast to the more wooded Chilterns to the east.

Open downland near Cuckhamsley Hill

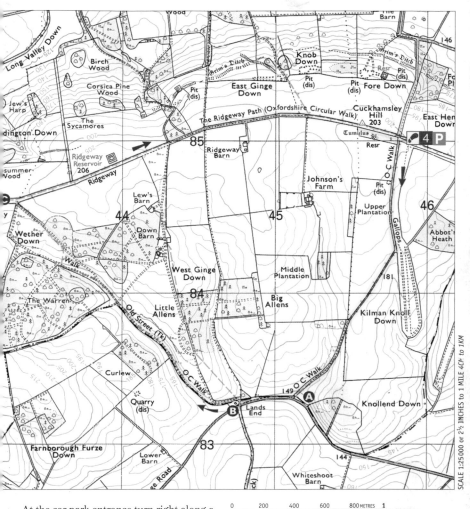

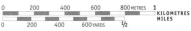

SCALE 1:25000 or 2½ INCHES to 1 MILE 4CP to 1KM

At the car park entrance turn right along a track, in the 'Public Right Of Way' direction shown on a footpath sign, across the downs. Immediately there are striking and expansive views, with the Thames Valley away in the distance on the left. The track gently descends and bears gradually right to reach a road **A**.

Turn right along the road for ¼ mile (400m), and just in front of a solitary house turn right **B** on to a track – there is a public bridleway sign ahead. At a fork take the left-hand grassy track – a blue waymark and plenty of white arrows indicate the correct route – and follow it for 1¼ miles (2km), through a shallow valley and then climbing gently through woodland up to the ridge ahead. Turn right **C** to join the Ridgeway and follow it for 1½ miles (2.4km) back to the start.

This is a fine scenic section with extensive views from both sides across what appears to be remote and uninhabited country, although later, Didcot power station and Harwell Laboratory are visible reminders of the 20th century. For the last ¼ mile (400m) the route passes between trees; Scutchamer Knob, a Saxon burial mound, is situated in the woodland on the right beside the car park.

●

Old Boars Hill

Start	Wootton, by church ¼ mile (400m) north of B4017
Distance	5 miles (8km)
Approximate time	2½ hours
Parking	Car park opposite Wootton church
Refreshments	Pub at Wootton, ¼ mile (400m) south of start
Ordnance Survey maps	Landranger 164 (Oxford), Pathfinder 1116, SP40/50 (Oxford)

The gentle wooded slopes of Old Boars Hill rise to 540ft (165m) to the south-west of Oxford, and from several vantage points on this undemanding walk there are grand views over the city's 'dreaming spires'. In addition there are some equally fine views over the Thames Valley, Chilterns and Berkshire Downs. Part of the route is across land owned by the Oxford Preservation Trust, set up in 1926 to preserve the city's attractive rural setting.

Turn right out of the car park opposite Wootton church and take the first turning on the right, signposted to Old Boars Hill. Follow the lane around first a right-hand and then a left-hand bend, and opposite a house turn left **A**, at a public footpath sign to Cumnor, along a track towards stables. Pass to the right of the stables, climbing several stiles in quick succession, and continue along the right-hand edge of a field, by a hedge on the right, to turn right over a stile in the field corner. Immediately climb another stile and continue along the left-hand edge of a field, by a wire fence and hedge on the right, gradually bearing right away from the field-edge to a stile.

Climb this, keep ahead over the next field, climb another stile and continue along the left-hand edge of a field, by a wire fence on the left, following the field-edge as it bends to the right. Turn left over a stile and follow a narrow path between gardens to rejoin the lane. Turn left uphill to reach a T-junction at the top **B**.

Bear right here through a gate to enter Jarn Mound and Wild Garden, owned by the Oxford Preservation Trust and constructed under the orders of Sir Arthur Evans, the famous archaeologist, in the early 1930s. The route continues to the right, but keep ahead and climb steps to the top of Jarn Mound for the view over Oxford, the Chilterns and the Berkshire Downs, which is now unfortunately partially obscured by trees. Retrace your steps to the gate and in front of it turn left along the stony path that passes to the right of a stone commemorating Sir Arthur Evans, and follow this path through the well-wooded garden as it bears left passing through a fence on to a lane. Turn right along the lane, Ridgeway, and at a junction keep ahead along Berkeley Road. At a kissing-gate by an Oxford Preservation Trust notice and collection box, turn left **C** and then turn right to follow a path across delightful, unimproved meadowland, at first keeping parallel to the lane on the right.

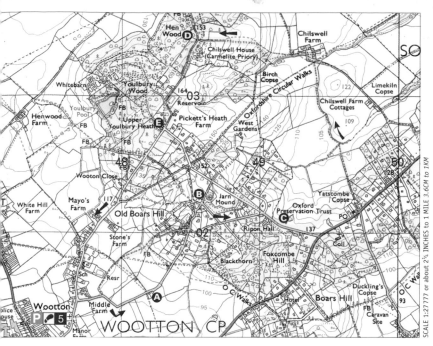

SCALE 1:27777 or about 2¾ INCHES to 1 MILE 3.6CM to 1KM

0	200	400	600	800 METRES	1	
						KILOMETRES
						MILES
0	200	400	600 YARDS		½	

Later the path bears left and passes to the left of a copse, fenced tree and bench. From here there is a fine view of Oxford. Head slightly downhill, making for the left edge of the belt of trees in front where there is a stile by a metal gate. Climb the stile and then turn left along the left-hand edge of a field, by a hedge on the left. Go through a metal gate, keep ahead across the next field and go through another metal gate. Continue along the right-hand edge of the next two fields, making for the farm buildings in front. Go through a metal gate on to a track, turn left and in front of the farm buildings turn sharp left along a concrete track. Pass to the left of a cottage and where the track turns right, keep ahead over a stile and continue along the left-hand edge of a field, by a line of trees and wire fence on the left.

In the field corner turn right to continue along the edge of the field, by a fence on the left, and near the top of a slight rise turn left over a stile and continue along a narrow path, between a wire fence on the left and hedges and scrub on the right, to join a track. Bear right along it – there are more fine views over Oxford to the right – heading across fields, later continuing between hedges to a T-junction of tracks **D**. Turn left along a tarmac track, which keeps along the left edge of Youlbury Wood, passing to the right of a reservoir. Take the first turning on the left, signposted to Oxford, but almost immediately turn right **E** through a gate into the Elizabeth Daryush Memorial Gardens, another piece of land owned by the Oxford Preservation Trust.

Follow a grassy path between trees and soon you reach a pond and benches, where there is a superb view ahead over the Berkshire Downs. Keep along a broad and obvious grassy path, and at a crossroads of paths about 100 yds (91m) in front of a house, bear right and continue down to a stile and public footpath sign at the bottom right-hand corner of the garden. Climb the stile to rejoin the tarmac track and turn left along it downhill. Later the track becomes a broader lane which continues through Wootton village to return to the start. ●

Dorchester and Wittenham Clumps

Dorchester and ✓
Wittenham Clumps

Start	Dorchester
Distance	4½ miles (7.2km)
Approximate time	2 hours
Parking	Dorchester
Refreshments	Pubs at Dorchester
Ordnance Survey maps	Landrangers 174 (Newbury & Wantage) and 164 (Oxford), Pathfinder 1136, SU49/59 (Abingdon)

An attractive village, an ancient abbey, riverside meadows, an Iron Age settlement, a medieval church, a prehistoric hillfort and fine woodland all feature in a remarkably varied walk for such a modest distance. The steep but short climb to Wittenham Clumps is rewarded with one of the finest views over the Thames Valley.

Before the Norman Conquest, Dorchester was a cathedral city, headquarters of the largest diocese in England, but the Normans transferred the see to Lincoln. On the site of the Saxon cathedral an Augustinian abbey was founded and the church, noted for its Norman nave and fine 13th- and 14th-century choir, largely survived the dissolution of the monasteries, although the rest of the monastic buildings were destroyed. Later Dorchester became an important staging post on the London–Oxford road – hence the large coaching inns in High Street – but is now bypassed and has reverted to being a sleepy but attractive backwater.

The walk starts at the southern end of High Street near the more southerly of the two entrances to the abbey grounds. Bear right off the main road along Bridge End and, just after passing the Catholic church on the left, bear right, at a public footpath sign to 'River and Wittenham', along a stony track – Wittenham Lane – between some picturesque cottages. After the last of the cottages continue along the left-hand edge of a field, by a hedge on the left. Climb a waymarked stile in the corner **A** and keep ahead alongside the Dyke Hills on the right, the ramparts of an Iron Age settlement that augmented the natural defences provided by the rivers Thame and Thames. Soon bear left to keep along the left-hand edge of a field and where the field-edge curves left, continue straight ahead, making for a stile in front. Climb this and walk across the meadow to reach the banks of the Thames just to the right of its confluence with the River Thame. Turn right alongside the Thames, pass through two gates and eventually follow it around a right-hand bend to Little Wittenham Bridge **B**.

Go through a gate to pass under the bridge, turn right and then sharp right again, go through another gate and cross Little Wittenham Bridge, actually three bridges in succession over different channels of the Thames. Continue along a tarmac path to Little Wittenham church and opposite it turn left over a stile into Little Wittenham Nature Reserve **C**.

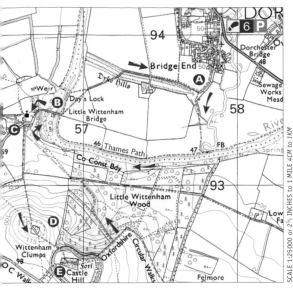

SCALE 1:25 000 or 2½ INCHES to 1 MILE 4CM to 1KM

Ahead is a fork; take the right-hand path which continues along the right-hand edge of a meadow, by a hedge on the right, making directly for Wittenham Clumps, part of the Sinodun Hills which rise abruptly above the surrounding flat terrain. Climb a stile and head steeply uphill across the open grassy hillside to Round Hill, the prominent tree-circle in front **D**. The steep climb is rewarded with a magnificent view of the Thames Valley, the river below and Dorchester Abbey clearly visible. Follow the boundary fence of the circle of trees around to the left and more views open up, including Didcot power station and the line of the Chilterns. The wooded hill immediately to the left is the Iron Age fort of Castle Hill, comprising circular ramparts and ditch. There is evidence that the fort continued to be occupied after the Roman conquest and might even have been used by the Saxons.

From Round Hill do not follow the obvious downhill path to the car park but turn sharp left along a downhill grassy path towards Castle Hill. Cross a track, continue to a stile, climb it and at a fork ahead bear right to head up through the outer defences of the fort. Walk across the grass to enter the trees which crown the fort, and by a waymarked post keep ahead to a T-junction of paths. Turn left **E** to continue through the impressive woodland that crowns Castle Hill.

On emerging from the trees bear slightly left to descend across the grassy slopes, dropping down an embankment to turn left over a stile. Continue downhill along the left-hand edge of a field, bordered by woods on the left, and climb a stile on the left about two-thirds of the way down. Follow the downhill path ahead along the right-hand side of a grassy ride through Little Wittenham Wood, and at the bottom bear slightly left on to a wide uphill track. Look out for where a yellow waymark directs you to bear right on to a path through trees. Pass beside a wooden barrier to a stony path ahead and turn left along the path to a stile. Climb it to emerge from the wood, turn half-right and head diagonally over a meadow to join the previous route in the far corner **C**, just in front of a stile.

Retrace your steps to Little Wittenham Bridge and after crossing the third and last of the succession of bridges **B**, go through a gate and turn half-left to follow a faint but discernible path across a meadow, heading in the direction of the tower of Dorchester Abbey. Go through another gate and continue along a hedge-and fence-lined path which passes through the Dyke Hills and then bears right to continue alongside them. Cross a track, keep along the right-hand edge of a field – still beside the 'dykes' on the right – and in the field corner turn left **A**, here rejoining the outward route again to retrace your steps to the start. ●

Widbrook Common and Cliveden Reach

Widbrook Common and Cliveden Reach

Start	Boulter's Lock, about ¾ mile (1.2km) north of Maidenhead Bridge on A4094
Distance	5½ miles (8.9km)
Approximate time	2½ hours
Parking	Boulter's Lock
Refreshments	Pubs and cafés at Cookham
Ordnance Survey maps	Landranger 175 (Reading & Windsor), Explorer 3 (Chiltern Hills South)

The walk to Cookham is mostly across flat, open meadow and marshland, with fine views across the surrounding countryside. After Cookham the route heads for the Thames and continues along Cliveden Reach, a beautiful stretch of the river below the glorious hanging woods of Cliveden, to return to Boulter's Lock.

Begin by walking away from the main road and take the path that leads from the far left-hand corner of the car park to a road. Turn left to a T-junction, turn right and, just after passing a road called The Pagoda, bear right **Ⓐ** along a path between fences. Where the path ends, cross a road, continue along the road ahead – Summerleaze Road – following it around a left-hand bend. Where the road turns sharply to the left **Ⓑ**, turn first right and then immediately turn left over a metal stile at a public footpath sign.

Follow the hedge-lined path ahead which bends right and continues by a wire fence bordering gravel works on the right, then bends left to a metal stile. Climb this, keep ahead to cross a footbridge over a small stream and continue along a grassy path by the stream on the right. On reaching a wider path just before a stile, turn right to cross first a footbridge and then a metal stile to a public footpath sign. Here keep ahead across the middle of a field, following the direction signposted

'Green-Way East', passing to the left of a line of trees and continuing to a public footpath sign at a gap in the hedge on the far side. Go through this gap and continue across the next field, bearing slightly right and then keeping by a wire fence on the right. Walk past the first footpath sign and continue to the second one by a metal stile in the field corner.

Climb the stile and bear right along a broad track. Ahead Cliveden House can be seen on its wooded cliff above the Thames and all around are wide views across flat meadowland. At a public footpath sign just before a metal gate, turn left and follow a path straight across a large field to climb a stile at the far end, here entering Widbrook Common, an area of pasture owned by the National Trust. Keep ahead to cross a footbridge and follow a path along the left-hand edge of the common, keeping parallel to a hedge and trees on the left, to a stile in the far corner. Climb the stile, keep along the right-hand edge of a field, by a metal fence on the right, and at the end of the field follow a public footpath sign to the right to continue along the left edge of the field, by trees on the left that border Strand Water. Keep along the left-hand edge of a second field and at the end of it cross a track, bear right to climb a stile and continue along the left-hand edge of a field, by a metal fence on the left. From here Cookham church tower is visible on the left; Cliveden House is ahead.

The route continues along an enclosed path which turns left to emerge eventually on to a drive at Cookham Moor on the western edge of the village. Turn right **C** to the war memorial and continue along High Street to a T-junction. Cookham is an attractive riverside village with a 12th-century church and many old buildings, some dating back to the 17th and 18th centuries. Stanley Spencer lived here for most of his life and many of his paintings were based on the local area. The Stanley Spencer Gallery is at the end of High Street.

At the T-junction turn right, in the Maidenhead direction, take the first turning on the left **D** – Mill Lane – and follow this winding lane for ½ mile (800km). On reaching some houses bear right, at a public footpath sign, along a hedge-lined path which curves left to a tarmac drive. Cross the drive and continue along the path opposite which winds through woodland, keeping parallel to the lane on the left, to reach the river **E**.

Turn right to follow the riverside path along Cliveden Reach, an exceptionally attractive stretch of the Thames, for

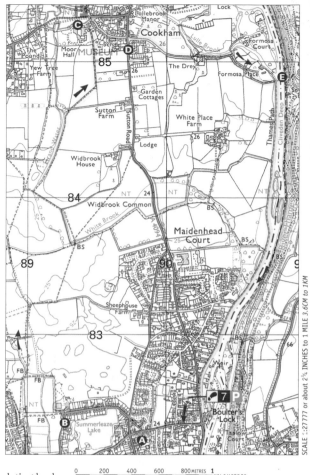

1½ miles (2.4km) back to Boulter's Lock. For most of the way the path is shady and tree-lined. To the right are extensive views across flat meadows to the wooded hills on the horizon, and to the left you pass below the hanging woods of Cliveden owned by the National Trust. Cliveden House, seen earlier on the walk, stands 200ft (61m) above the river. The present house – the third on the site and built by Barry in 1851 – became the property of the Astor family and was associated with the political intrigues of the 'Cliveden Set' in the 1920s and 1930s, and later with the Profumo scandal of 1963. The path eventually emerges on to the road opposite the car park at Boulter's Lock. ●

Windsor and Eton

Start	Windsor
Distance	5½ miles (8.9km). Shorter version 3 miles (4.8km)
Approximate time	2½ hours (1½ hours for shorter version)
Parking	Windsor
Refreshments	Pubs, cafés and restaurants at Windsor and Eton, pubs at Eton Wick
Ordnance Survey maps	Landranger 175 (Reading & Windsor), Pathfinder 1173, SU87/97 (Windsor)

Riverside meadows, the playing-fields of Eton and views of Windsor Castle and Eton College are the main ingredients of this flat and easy walk. Towards the end there is a particularly memorable view of Windsor Castle rising majestically above the opposite bank of the Thames. Leave plenty of time to explore the many historic attractions of Windsor.

From the banks of the Thames, Castle Hill winds up to Windsor Castle, the largest castle in Britain and a royal residence for over 900 years. It was begun by William the Conqueror in the late 11th century as one of a chain of castles defending the approaches to London, but over the centuries successive monarchs have remodelled and added to it – notably

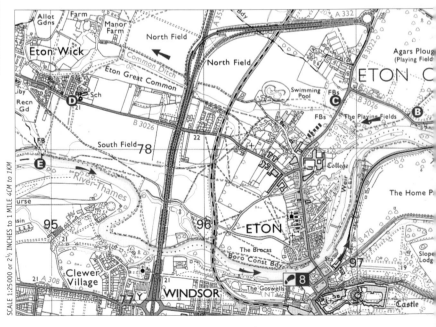

Henry II (who rebuilt the original circular keep), Henry III, Henry VIII, Charles II and George IV. Much of its present appearance dates from a particularly extensive programme of restoration and rebuilding carried out by George IV in the early 19th century. St George's Chapel, begun by Edward IV in 1478, is a masterpiece of Perpendicular Gothic architecture and contains many royal tombs. Despite all the additions and modernisation, Windsor still retains the basic plan of a Norman castle, with its varied buildings grouped around the massive 12th-century (though much restored) shell keep that dominates all the views of the fortress.

Although the castle is inevitably the major draw, Windsor has other attractions, including an elegant 17th-century guildhall (partly built by Wren) and the Royalty and Empire Exhibition in the Central Station. The station was built in 1897 to commemorate Queen Victoria's Diamond Jubilee and nowadays houses a display which imaginatively brings to life the celebrations of that year and the events and people of Victoria's long reign.

Across the river is Eton, whose

attractive High Street leads to the red brick buildings of Eton College, founded by Henry VI in 1440 but, like Windsor Castle, added to over the centuries. Many Prime Ministers, from the Elder Pitt to Harold Macmillan, have been educated there.

Start at the pedestrianised bridge over the Thames that links Windsor and Eton, and with your back to the river and facing Windsor Castle, turn left down steps on to Thames Side to walk alongside the river. After passing the Donkey House

pub go through a metal gate. Continue along a tarmac path between railings – Romney Walk – passing to the left of the station, and on meeting a tarmac track turn left along it to enter Crown Estate land. The track keeps alongside the railway line to reach a boatyard by Romney Lock.

Climb a stile immediately in front and walk along the riverside path to follow the Thames around a right-hand bend, passing under a railway bridge and continuing towards a road bridge. To the right are fine views across Home Park to the castle. Just before the road bridge turn sharp right across the grass to reach the road at the end of white railings, turn sharp left to cross the bridge, continue along the road for about 100 yds (91m) and turn left Ⓐ on to a track that keeps along the left edge of Datchet golf-course, by trees and undergrowth bordering the river on the left.

In the far corner of the golf-course continue, by a wire fence on the right, to a public footpath sign just in front of a railway bridge. Turn left to pass under the bridge, go through a kissing-gate and then bear slightly left to continue across rough meadowland. Cross a footbridge, climb two stiles in quick succession, and walk along a narrow path to climb a third stile and emerge on to the riverbank, just to the left of a boathouse. Keep ahead along the tarmac track to a road, bear left along it and then continue along the path parallel to it. Opposite a public footpath sign turn left over a footbridge Ⓑ to follow a clear, well-surfaced track across part of the playing-fields of Eton College. Just in front of a brick bridge, turn sharp right to continue along the track which curves to the left and passes through a kissing-gate by a lodge on to a road Ⓒ.

For the shorter version of the walk, turn left along the road, passing Eton College and continue along Eton High Street to the starting point.

For the full walk, cross the road and go through a gate in the fence opposite, at a public footpath sign. Keep ahead across more playing-fields to cross a footbridge by another public footpath sign. Continue along the track ahead, by a line of trees on the left, and at the end of the playing-fields keep ahead along a track to emerge in front of cottages. Here bear slightly left along a tarmac drive, go through a gate and at a T-junction ahead turn right. Keep left at a fork, continue along a tarmac track and pass under a railway bridge. The tarmac track now continues as a rough track across fields, bending first to the left and then to the right to pass under a road bridge. The track bends right and left again to continue across fields to a public footpath sign at a crossroads of tracks.

Turn left, cross a footbridge over Common Ditch and turn right to head across a meadow, keeping roughly parallel with the ditch on the right, to a metal gate by a public footpath sign. Go through it on to a lane, turn left, and at a T-junction turn right on the edge of Eton Wick. Turn left beside the Greyhound pub to reach another T-junction **D**. Turn right and almost immediately turn left, at a public footpath sign, along a narrow but straight, clearly defined path across meadows. Keep ahead at a crossroads of paths and on the far side of the meadows bear left to the river ahead **E**.

Turn left and follow the winding river for about 1½ miles (2.4km) back to the start, passing under both road and railway bridges again. The grand finale to the walk is the majestic view of Windsor Castle, its walls and towers rising above the opposite bank. On reaching the end of the meadows keep ahead, first along a tarmac drive and then along a road, to the bottom end of Eton High Street. Turn right to cross the bridge back into Windsor. ●

Windsor Castle, majestic above the Thames

*Siern
13.2.00
Clayfield,12.2.00*

Abingdon and Sutton Courtenay

Start	Abingdon, on south side of bridge
Distance	7 miles (11.3km)
Approximate time	3½ hours
Parking	Abingdon
Refreshments	Pubs and cafés at Abingdon, pub at Sutton Courtenay, pub on A415 to north-east of Culham
Ordnance Survey maps	Landranger 164 (Oxford), Pathfinder 1136, SU49/59 (Abingdon)

Much of this route involves long stretches of pleasant walking by the riverside, following the Thames as it makes a large curve to the east and south of Abingdon. The terrain is flat throughout, the views are wide and extensive, and there is an opportunity to visit two villages as well as to explore Abingdon itself, a fine historic town.

Abingdon has always been an important crossing-point on the Thames. The bridge and causeway which link it to Culham were built by the local guild of merchants in the 15th century, to improve communications and overcome the problem of flooding, and thus ensure the town's continued prosperity. Of the great Benedictine abbey, once one of the wealthiest in the country, only fragments survive but Abingdon possesses some impressive churches and a particularly grand and dignified 17th-century town hall, possibly influenced by Wren. There are also attractive views of the town from the opposite bank of the river.

Begin by walking across the grass to the river, turn left along the riverside path

and follow it for about 1¾ miles (2.8km) to Culham. This is a pleasant stretch of the Thames across unspoilt riverside meadows, and the path is tree-shaded in places. At times Didcot power station can be glimpsed ahead. There are several stiles and gates to negotiate, and a footbridge

Sutton Courtenay

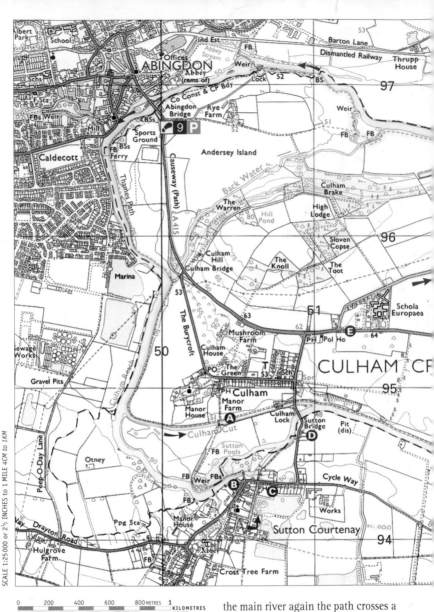

SCALE 1:25000 or 2½ INCHES to 1 MILE 4CM to 1KM

0	200	400	600	800 METRES	1
					KILOMETRES
					MILES
0	200	400	600 YARDS	½	

over Back Water. Eventually the path bends to the left to follow Culham Cut, an arm of the Thames. To the left the picturesque grouping of the manor house and church at Culham can be seen across the meadows.

At a footbridge turn left to visit Culham; the route continues by turning right **A** over the footbridge and taking the path ahead across fields. On meeting the main river again the path crosses a footbridge above a weir, continues through trees and then follows the curve of the river sharply to the left to cross three successive footbridges above weirs. Keep ahead along a shady riverside path which bends sharply right and passes through a metal kissing-gate into Sutton Courtenay **B**. This attractive village of brick and half-timbered cottages and houses – some thatched – has a large tree-lined green and a fine medieval church that retains some Norman work. Two

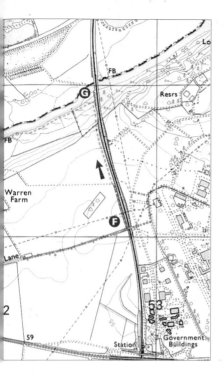

keep ahead along the road for ¼ mile (400m) to a T-junction. Turn right, in the Dorchester direction, along the main road – there is a path beside it – and take the first side-road on the left **E**, Thame Lane, signposted to the European School. The road soon curves right and continues in a straight line for 1 mile (1.6km), becoming a narrow lane after passing the school entrance and then a rough track after passing Warren Farm. All around there are wide views across the Oxford Plain, and to the right Wittenham Clumps can be seen in the foreground, with the line of the Chilterns on the horizon.

Just before reaching a railway bridge turn left **F**, at a public footpath sign to Abingdon, and keep along the right-hand edge of fields beside a railway line in its cutting on the right. At a field corner keep ahead, go through a hedge gap and head down to climb a stile. Continue downhill, now below a railway embankment instead of above a cutting, and in the bottom corner of the field turn left **G** to continue along the field edge. The River Thames is just beyond the line of trees and bushes on the right; keep beside the river along the right-hand edge of fields. The path on this section of the walk is narrow, uneven and likely to be overgrown. Follow the field edge as it curves left, away from the river, and look out for the point where a path turns right to head through trees and scrub to cross two footbridges. Bear right through the trees to emerge on the edge of rough meadowland and turn left to follow a path across the meadow. Cross another footbridge and follow the narrow path ahead along the right-hand edge of the meadow, by trees on the right.

Later you rejoin the Thames and turn left to follow it back to Abingdon Bridge. This is an attractive finale on a well-surfaced path, passing Abingdon Lock and continuing across meadows with good views of the town ahead. Pass under the bridge and the car park is to the left. ●

famous men are buried here: Herbert Asquith and George Orwell.

Either bear left if wishing to omit the 'loop' through the village or turn right along Church Street. Continue along a tarmac path, at a public footpath sign, passing the George and Dragon pub and the church, and turn left along a narrow tarmac path, between a cottage on the right and the churchyard wall on the left. Pass through a metal barrier on to a track, and at a T-junction of tracks turn left along a wide concrete drive, still alongside the churchyard wall, and follow the drive to a road **C**, rejoining the shorter route which omitted the village. Cross the road, climb over a stile and continue along the concrete drive which bears right to another stile. Climb it, continue along the left-hand edge of a meadow, soon rejoining the riverbank and following it to Sutton Bridge. Just before the bridge look out for a public footpath sign on the right, where you pass through a gate on to a road **D**.

Turn left, cross first Sutton Bridge and then another one over Culham Cut and

Aston Hill and Drayton Beauchamp

Aston Hill and Drayton Beauchamp

Start	Forestry Commission's Aston Hill car park
Distance	5½ miles (8.9km)
Approximate time	2½ hours
Parking	Aston Hill
Refreshments	Pub at Bucklandwharf
Ordnance Survey maps	Landranger 165 (Aylesbury & Leighton Buzzard), Explorer 2 (Chiltern Hills North)

From the thickly wooded slopes of Aston Hill, a fine viewpoint over the Vale of Aylesbury, the route descends to the flatter land of the vale and continues across fields to reach the disused Wendover arm of the Grand Union Canal at Drayton Beauchamp. An attractive and tranquil stroll by the canal – where at first the bed is dry but water soon appears – is followed by a steady climb through woodland to return to the start.

Begin by walking away from the road and at the far end of the car park bear right through a wooden barrier to join a broad track. Turn left along the track, climb a stile beside a gate to the left of a house and continue along a downhill path through a lovely area of woodland. The path continues more steeply downhill along the left inside-edge of woodland, by a wire fence on the left, to reach a lane.

Turn right, and at a public footpath sign turn left **Ⓐ** along a narrow tree-lined path and continue along the left-hand edge of fields to a track. Turn left along the track, and in front of the entrance to Drayton Manor turn right and continue along the track to cross a bridge over a dual carriageway, then keep ahead to a road. Cross the road and continue along the right-hand edge of a field, by a hedge on the right, following the field-edge around right and left bends to reach the next road. Turn right along the road and

then turn sharp left **Ⓑ** over a stile at a public footpath sign, to continue through an area of scrub and bushes to another stile. Climb it and turn right to walk across grass, between farm buildings on the left and bushes on the right. Bear left

Tranquil canal scene near Bucklandwharf

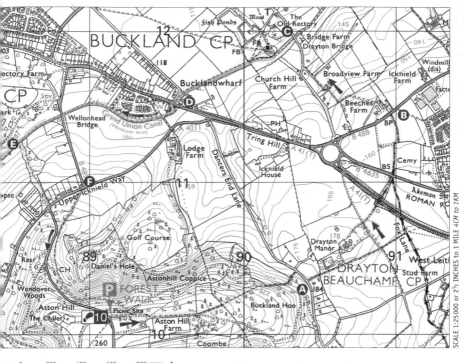

SCALE 1:25000 or 2½ INCHES to 1 MILE 4CM to 1KM

0   200   400   600   800 METRES   1
                                    KILOMETRES
                                    MILES
0   200   400   600 YARDS   ½

around the end of the farm buildings and head across to a drive. Cross the drive, continue straight across a field, climb a stile on the far side and turn left alongside a hedge and wire fence on the left. On reaching a fence with a yellow waymark turn right and keep beside the fence to a stile. Climb this, keep ahead to walk along a concrete drive, climb another stile and continue along the tarmac drive to a lane.

Turn right along the lane, cross a bridge over a disused canal and immediately turn left over a stile **C**. Head down the embankment and turn right to walk along the path above the dry bed of the canal. This was the Wendover arm of the Grand Union Canal, constructed in the 1790s but never a commercial success. A little further on, water appears in the canal and at this point a stile on the right enables you to visit Drayton Beauchamp church: climb the stile, walk along a path to climb another stile and continue across a field to the mainly 15th-century church.

The route continues beside the canal and to the left is a pleasant view of Aston Hill Woods. At the first bridge climb a stile, cross a drive and continue by the canal to the road bridge at Bucklandwharf. Turn left over the bridge and turn right **D** to continue along the opposite bank of the canal, a particularly attractive part of the walk. About 200 yds (183m) after passing under the next road bridge, turn left over a stile **E** and follow a path quite steeply uphill through a belt of woodland to climb another stile on to a road.

Turn left, and opposite the turning to Aylesbury turn right **F** over a stile, at a public footpath sign, turn right again and head gently uphill between a wire fence on the left and a hedge on the right. Where both the fence and hedge end, keep ahead along the edge of a golf course, following a line of short, red-topped posts. After passing in front of the clubhouse the path enters woodland. Continue uphill through this attractive woodland to reach a track in front of a wire fence and turn right along the track to return to the start. ●

Dunstable Downs

Dunstable Downs

Start	Robertson Corner, Dunstable Downs visitor centre
Distance	4½ miles (7.2km)
Approximate time	2½ hours
Parking	Dunstable Downs visitor centre
Refreshments	Kiosk at visitor centre, pubs at Whipsnade
Ordnance Survey maps	Pathfinder 1095, TL01/11 (Harpenden), Explorer 2 (Chiltern Hills North)

The Dunstable Downs form part of the steep western escarpment of the Chiltern range, and from their open, grassy slopes there are extensive views over the Vale of Aylesbury and further afield towards the flat country bordering the East Midlands and East Anglia. From the visitor centre on top of the downs the route heads across pleasant, undulating country to Whipsnade Heath, passing by the unusual 'Tree Cathedral' at Whipsnade before returning to the edge of the escarpment. The finale is a splendid 1-mile (1.6km) ramble along the crest of the downs with grand views all the while. This is a well-waymarked walk as it follows one of Bedfordshire County Council's 'Circular Routes'.

From the visitor centre turn right along the road to the point where it forks at Robertson Corner. A monument here reveals how this road junction got its name: two brothers called Robertson were killed in World War I and a third brother gave the surrounding land to the National Trust as a memorial. At the fork take the left-hand road, pass the entrance to Kensworth Quarry, and after ¹/₂ mile (800m) – just after passing a house and before reaching a radio mast – turn left through a gap in a hedge **A**.

Walk along the left-hand edge of a field, by a hedge on the left, and in the field corner keep ahead through trees and then continue along the right-hand edge of the next field, by a hedge on the right, heading downhill. Just before reaching the bottom corner of the field, turn right and then immediately left to walk along a track, keeping right at a fork and continuing, by a hedge and line of trees on the left, towards Kensworth Quarry. Look out for a yellow waymark which directs you to the right to continue along a pleasant path through a belt of trees. Climb a stile on the edge of the trees, keep ahead across a sloping field, just below the steepest part of the slope on the left, climb another stile and bear slightly right to head downhill across the next field to climb a stile in the bottom corner.

Turn right to walk along the right-hand edge of a field, by a hedge on the right. Climb a stile, pass to the left of a barn, turn right over another stile in front of a gate and then turn left to continue in the same direction as before, along a track that heads uphill to a cattle-grid. Keep along a hedge-lined track and, just before reaching a barn and metal gate, turn left

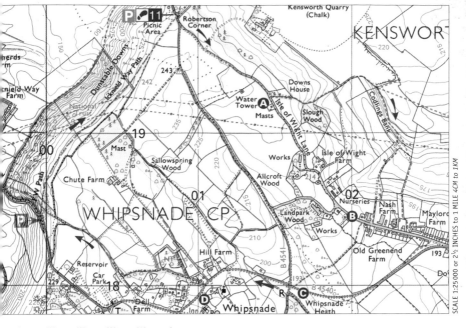

SCALE 1:25000 or 2½ INCHES to 1 MILE 4CM to 1KM

over a stile in the hedge and continue along a narrow path, climbing a stile on to a road. Turn right, and at a public footpath sign turn left **B** over a stile and walk across the middle of a field, passing a solitary tree, to a stile. Climb the stile and walk along a narrow path, between a hedge on the left and wire fence on the right. Pass between a wooden barrier on the edge of trees and continue through woodland to go through another barrier on the far side. Keep ahead across Whipsnade Heath car park to a road **C**.

Turn right, keep ahead at a crossroads and continue along the road into Whipsnade village – the road is busy but there is a verge for most of the way. Continue along the right-hand edge of the spacious green, opposite Whipsnade's brick church, and at a sign for 'Tree Cathedral' turn right **D** along a tarmac drive. Bear right to continue along a track and go through a gate into the grounds of Whipsnade Tree Cathedral, a variety of trees planted in the shape of a cathedral. This was created in 1931 by Edmund

Blyth and was inspired by the building of Liverpool Cathedral, his experiences in World War I and the loss of friends killed in that war. He bequeathed it to the National Trust.

The route continues along the left edge of the 'cathedral grounds' to a stile. Climb the stile, keep along the left-hand edge of a field to climb another stile and continue to a T-junction of paths. Turn right, following both Circular Route and Icknield Way signs, along a pleasantly tree- and hedge-lined path to reach the edge of the escarpment. Ahead is a magnificent view over the Vale of Aylesbury, with the line of the Chilterns stretching away to the left. The path bears right, but almost immediately turn left along a narrow path to a finger-post and turn right, in the Dunstable Downs direction, to a gate.

Go through the gate on to open downland for the superb finale. As you continue gently uphill across the slopes of the downs, there are extensive views over flat country to the left and a dramatic view ahead of the gently curving escarpment. The path leads directly back to the car park and visitor centre. ●

Goring

Start	Goring
Distance	6 miles (9.7km)
Approximate time	3 hours
Parking	Goring
Refreshments	Pubs and cafés at Goring
Ordnance Survey maps	Landrangers 175 (Reading & Windsor) and 174 (Newbury & Wantage), Pathfinders 1155 SU48/58 (Wantage (East) & Didcot (South)) and 1172, SU67/77 (Reading), Explorer 3 (Chiltern Hills South)

From the banks of the River Thames this walk follows an undulating route in an arc to the north, east and south of Goring, passing through a succession of attractive wooded areas. Near the end there are superb views looking across the Thames Valley to the Berkshire Downs. Expect some muddy stretches in the woods, but all the climbs are modest and gradual.

Goring stands on the eastern bank of the Thames where the river cuts through the Goring Gap between the Chilterns and Berkshire Downs. The bridge linking Goring and Streatley on the western bank dates only from the 19th century; before that the river had to be crossed by ferry.

Start by the bridge over the Thames and walk up High Street through the village. Cross a railway bridge, keep ahead **A** along a tarmac drive in front of houses, and where the drive bends slightly right turn left along a fenced tarmac path to a road. Keep ahead through a modern housing area and where the road ends, continue along a tarmac path, then turn right through a fence gap on to a road.

Cross the road, and at a public footpath sign take the narrow path opposite between fences. Climb a stile and turn right to climb another one a little further on. Follow a narrow path along the bottom edge of a sloping field, by a hedge and wire fence on the left, climb a stile and continue along an enclosed, wooded path, beside garden fences on the left and then below sloping woodland on the right, to emerge on to a lane **B**. Turn right and almost immediately turn left, at a public footpath sign to Beech Lane and Woodcote, along a narrow, enclosed path, later keeping along the left edge of woodland. To the left are fine open views across to the Berkshire Downs. The path bears right to continue uphill through Wroxhills Wood to a crossroads of paths.

Climb the stile opposite and follow a narrow but obvious path through the trees, keeping in a fairly straight line, to emerge on to a track in the far corner of the wood. Turn right along this hedge-and tree-lined track and at the point where it becomes a tarmac drive, turn right **C**, at a public footpath sign, along the track which heads straight across fields and descends to a waymarked stile. Do not climb the stile but turn left and continue gently downhill along a track to go through a metal gate on to a road. Turn left and after about 100 yds (91m) bear

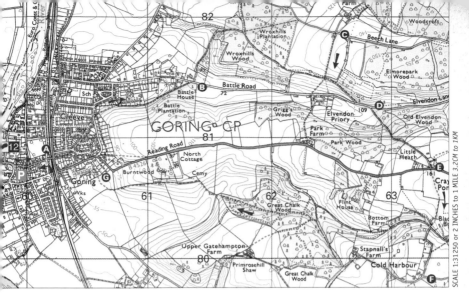

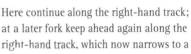

SCALE 1:31250 or 2 INCHES to 1 MILE 3.2CM to 1KM

right **D** along a track through Old Elvendon Wood. Head uphill to emerge from the trees, continue along a track to a road **E**, cross the road and climb a stile opposite, at a public footpath sign to Cold Harbour. Bear slightly left and follow a faint path diagonally across a field. On the far side pass through a hedge gap to continue between a hedge on the left and a wire fence on the right. The path curves right and left, following the contours of the field on the right. After climbing a stile, you re-enter woodland and descend to a track in the valley bottom. Cross this, take the uphill path ahead to a house, turn left along another track in front of the house and follow this tarmac track as it curves right and continues to a lane **F**.

Turn right along the narrow lane, passing to the left of Coldharbour Farm and follow the lane to Stapnall's Farm. Just in front of the farm turn left through a metal gate, walk along the right-hand edge of a field, turn right through a gate in the field corner and then turn left to continue along a tree-lined path. Go through a gate into woodland, then turn right along a track that continues through the mainly coniferous Great Chalk Wood. Head gently downhill to reach a waymarked gate: do not go through it but turn left to keep along the track to a fork.

Here continue along the right-hand track; at a later fork keep ahead again along the right-hand track, which now narrows to a path and heads gently downhill, passing a waymarked post and continuing to a stile.

Climb the stile, keep ahead through bushes, and climb another stile on the edge of open country. Walk uphill along the right-hand edge of a field, by a hedge on the right, turn left in the field corner and continue along the top edge of the field to climb a half-hidden stile in the far corner. On this section of the walk there are impressive views over the Thames Valley to the Berkshire Downs. Keep along the top edge of the next field, later descending to pass through a hedge gap into the next field and continuing as far as a stile in the hedge on the right.

Climb the stile, bear slightly left to walk across the middle of a playing-field, climb a stile at the far end and continue along a tarmac path to a road on the edge of a modern housing estate **G**. Walk along the road, turn left to a T-junction, then turn right to another T-junction and turn left.

At the next T-junction, by the Queen's Arms, turn right and then turn left over the railway bridge to return to the start. ●

Amersham and Chalfont St Giles

Start	Amersham
Distance	6½ miles (10.5km)
Approximate time	3½ hours
Parking	Amersham
Refreshments	Pubs and cafés at Amersham, pubs and café at Chalfont St Giles
Ordnance Survey maps	Landranger 176 (West London), Explorer 3 (Chiltern Hills South)

A gradual and undulating climb out of Amersham, across fields and through areas of woodland above the lovely Misbourne valley, is followed by an equally gentle descent into the village of Chalfont St Giles, noted for its associations with John Milton. The return route to Amersham follows the well-waymarked South Bucks Way along the bottom of the valley.

Amersham's long and wide main street is lined by brick-built and timber-framed cottages and old coaching inns, the latter a reflection of the town's importance in the days of the stagecoach. In the centre of the street stands the 17th-century market hall and nearby is the large, mainly 15th-century church, heavily restored in the Victorian period.

Start by the market hall and walk eastwards along Broadway, passing to the right of the church. Opposite Tesco's car park turn right **Ⓐ** through a gate into Bury Farm, at public footpath and South Bucks Way signs, bear left along a track and follow it under the bypass and along the right-hand edge of a meadow, by a hedge on the right.

Turn right over a stile beside a metal gate **Ⓑ** and bear left to follow a steadily ascending path across a field, making for the trees ahead. Climb a stile into Rodger's Wood, continue gently uphill through it,

climb another stile on the other side and continue straight across two fields, bearing left along a track on reaching the edge of the second field. To the left are fine views over the Misbourne valley. Continue along the right-hand edge of fields and, just before reaching the next area of woodland, turn right over a stile and bear left, following the direction of a yellow waymark, diagonally across a field – there is no obvious path – making for a stile just to the left of the field corner. Climb the stile and continue across the next field, keeping to the left of a short and broken stretch of former hedge-line, to pick up a discernible path and head downhill towards farm buildings, by a wire fence on the right.

Just before reaching the bottom of the field bear left away from the wire fence to climb a stile, go down steps and keep ahead, passing to the left of barns, to a narrow lane. Turn right along the lane,

and at a public footpath sign to Hodgemoor turn left through a metal gate and head uphill along a track, by a hedge and trees on the right. At a fork take the left-hand track which continues uphill along the left edge of woodland, then becomes a narrow path which keeps ahead, between a wire fence on the left and a line of trees on the right, to a stile to the left of a gate. Climb the stile and continue along the track ahead, passing between houses and heading gently downhill through woodland to reach a road **C**.

Continue straight ahead along Dodds Lane down into Chalfont St Giles, keeping to the left of the green to a T-junction in the attractive village centre. The large green is lined by cottages and shops, and just off it is the secluded medieval church. A ¼-mile (400m) detour to the right brings you to Milton's Cottage, where the poet came in 1665 to escape from the Great Plague of London. During the year that he spent here he finished *Paradise Lost* and began *Paradise Regained*.

At the T-junction immediately turn sharp left **D** along a track, at a South Bucks Way sign, passing to the right of a house. Continue along this pleasant tree-lined track, taking the right-hand track at a fork and keeping along the right edge of woodland, by a fence on the right. At the end of the trees continue first along a fence-lined path, then along a track to the right of houses, to a lane. Keep ahead along the lane and where it bends left **E**, continue along a partially hedge- and tree-lined track, which later narrows to a path and keeps along the right inside-edge of woodland to a stile.

Climb the stile to leave the wood and for the rest of the walk there are attractive, open views over the Misbourne valley. Continue along the left-hand edge of a field, by a wire fence on the left, follow the field-edge around to the right for a short distance, then turn left over a stile and keep along the right-hand edge of a field, by a hedge and wire fence on the right, to climb another stile on to a lane. Cross the lane, climb the stile opposite and walk across a field, bearing slightly right to climb a stile in a hedge. Continue in the same direction across the next field, then keep by a wire fence bordering trees on the right to reach a stile in the far corner. Climb the stile and keep along the right-hand edge of the next field, by a wire fence and hedge on the right. Climb another stile and continue along the right-hand edge of the next field. Where the hedge bends right, keep ahead in a straight line across the field, then pick up and keep by a hedge on the left to continue to a stile in the corner of the field.

Climb the stile and continue straight across the field ahead. The path bears slightly round to the left to meet a hedge by a stile, where you pick up a track to rejoin the outward route and retrace your steps to Amersham. ●

Chalfont St Giles

Cookham, Winter Hill and Cock Marsh

Start	National Trust car park at Cookham Moor, ¼ mile (400m) west of Cookham village centre
Distance	6½ miles (10.5km)
Approximate time	3½ hours
Parking	Cookham Moor. Alternatively, car park in Cookham village
Refreshments	Pubs and cafés at Cookham, pubs at Cookham Dean, pub by river opposite Bourne End
Ordnance Survey maps	Landranger 175 (Reading & Windsor), Explorer 3 (Chiltern Hills South)

This walk embraces woodland, marsh and meadow; extensive views over the Thames Valley; pleasant and easy riverside walking, and an attractive village. The first part of the route to Winter Hill is undulating, though none of the uphill sections are lengthy or strenuous; the last part along the banks of the Thames by Cock Marsh is flat and makes for a relaxing finale. This is very much Stanley Spencer country: the artist spent most of his life in Cookham, and the village and surrounding area were the inspiration for many of his paintings.

With your back to the road take the path that leads from the far left-hand corner of the car park. At a footpath sign in front of the gate to Pound Farm, turn left into the trees and cross a footbridge. Climb the stile ahead and continue along the right-hand edge of a field, by a wire fence and trees on the right, following the field edge as it curves to the right. About 50 yds (46m) before the end of the field, bear left and head slightly uphill to a stile and footpath sign.

Climb the stile and continue uphill along a narrow, enclosed path. At the top, just before reaching a road, turn right Ⓐ, at a public footpath sign, along a broad track. Climb another stile and continue along the top edge of a golf-course, by a

wire fence on the left, to a railway bridge. From this elevated and open section there are grand views over Cookham and the Thames Valley. Turn left over the bridge and keep straight ahead along a grassy path, still across the golf-course, heading uphill and making for the corner of the hedge in front. Keep by a hedge and wire fence on the left, and at the fence corner bear left to climb a stile and turn left along a path between wire fences to a road. Cross the road, climb the stile opposite and continue along the right-hand edge of a field, by a fence on the right, to climb another stile. Bear right along an enclosed path, climb a stile on to a road and keep ahead along Alleyns Lane, heading downhill. At the bottom, by some picturesque black-and-white cottages, turn right along Dean Lane and take the first turning on the left **B**, Warners Hill, to head steeply uphill. At a T-junction by Uncle Tom's Cabin, cross the road and turn right along a path across Harding's Green, a National Trust property. The path runs parallel to the road on the right and at the end of the green rejoins it. The road bends right, then bears left; almost immediately turn right **C**, at a public footpath sign, and head diagonally across Cookham Dean village green towards the Inn on the Green pub sign. Here take the tarmac drive ahead to the pub.

Immediately at the entrance to the pub turn right, at a footpath sign, on to a narrow path through trees and bushes to a stile. Climb the stile, continue across a field, climb another stile and head downhill across the next field to a public footpath sign at the bottom. Bear slightly right to continue along the right-hand edge of a field, by a wire fence on the right, to a road **D**. Either turn right along the road for ¼ mile (400m) to a junction or use the parallel path just inside the woodland on the left, part of the Woodland Trust's Bisham Woods property.

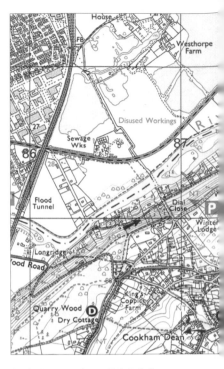

At the junction bear slightly left to cross Quarry Wood Road and take the path opposite between fences. At a T-junction of paths turn left, and then turn right, at a public footpath sign, to continue through delightful woodland, keeping a look-out for the regular white arrows on trees that indicate the route. Later the path keeps by a wire fence and after that by a wall on the right. When the wall ends continue along a drive and, where the drive bends

---

The view from Winter Hill

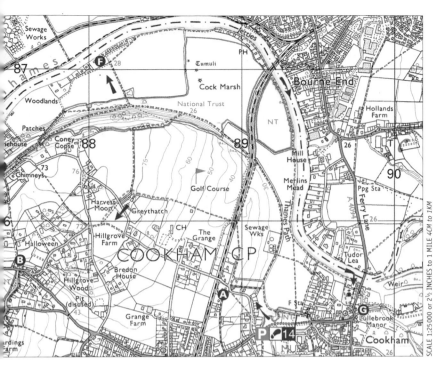

SCALE 1:25 000 or 2½ INCHES to 1 MILE 4CM to 1KM

right to a road, turn left on to a narrow path through trees to emerge at the parking area on top of Winter Hill ❺. From here there is a superb and extensive view over the Thames Valley looking towards Marlow, with the Chilterns visible on the horizon.

Continue along the road that runs along the top of the hill and shortly after passing a turning on the left, Gibraltar Lane, bear left along a downhill track. Climb a stile and continue along the track, descending gently and keeping on the main track all the while. At the bottom the track bends left to a stile. Climb over it, keep ahead across a field, and at the end of the field turn right ❻, at a public footpath sign, to continue along a grassy path to the river.

Keep along the bank of the Thames for 1½ miles (2.4km), following it around a right-hand bend to Cookham. The path hugs the riverbank all the while, crossing attractive riverside meadows and with fine views to the right across the open expanses of Cock Marsh to Winter Hill. Keep by the river almost to Cookham

Bridge, but at the end of a tarmac section, turn right by the fence of a large white house and go through a metal kissing-gate into the churchyard. Walk through the churchyard, passing the beautiful 12th-century church, go through a gate at the far end, turn left to the road and turn right through the village.

Cookham is an attractive village with a splendid position by the riverside and a wealth of old buildings, many of them dating back to the 17th and 18th centuries. The artist Stanley Spencer lived here for most of his life.

At a junction turn right ❼, in front of the Stanley Spencer Gallery, along High Street and just after passing the war memorial continue along a raised causeway to the left of the road above the open, grassy area of Cookham Moor. This causeway has been in existence since 1770. In front of a brick bridge turn right, go down some steps and head across the grass to return to the car park. ●

Great Hampden
and Little Hampden

Start	Cockshoots Wood car park and picnic area. Turn off A413 about 1¾ miles (2.8km) south of Wendover along lane signposted to Cobblers Hill, car park is ½ mile (800m) along this lane
Distance	6½ miles (10.5km)
Approximate time	3 hours
Parking	Cockshoots Wood
Refreshments	Pub at Little Hampden
Ordnance Survey maps	Landranger 165 (Aylesbury & Leighton Buzzard), Explorer 2 (Chiltern Hills North)

Apart from one fairly steep climb near the end, this is a gently undulating walk through a peaceful, rolling and well-wooded landscape in the heart of the Chilterns. The route passes two remote and interesting churches at Great Hampden and Little Hampden.

The first part of the walk can be confusing as there are lots of paths through Cockshoots Wood; follow directions carefully and look out for the frequent white arrows on tree trunks. With your back to the lane, turn right across the picnic area and go through a gap in a fence – indicated by a white arrow – to take a rather indistinct and overgrown path ahead through rough, tall grass, making for a tree ahead with a white arrow. Here bear slightly left to enter woodland, then turn right (arrows on two trees indicate the direction) to head uphill, bearing gradually right all the time.

On joining another path bear left, following the direction of an arrow, and continue gently uphill, winding through attractive woodland and keeping on the main path all the while. At a fork follow a white arrow to take the left-hand path; at another fork keep ahead – this time ignoring a white arrow to the left – and

eventually bear slightly right, by a wire fence on the right, to reach a track opposite a house. Turn right along the track to reach a lane and public bridleway sign **A**.

Turn left along the lane, passing to the left of a farm and keep along the right-hand lane at a fork. At a public footpath sign turn left through a metal gate. Walk along a grassy, hedge-lined path and, emerging into a field, turn right to continue along the right-hand edge of the field, by a hedge on the right. The path later keeps along the right inside-edge of woodland. On leaving the wood bear right along a track and then bear left, at a white arrow, to go gently downhill along the right-hand edge of a field, by a hedge and trees on the right. Go through a hedge gap in the field corner and continue downhill across the middle of a field to a road.

Cross the road, take the lane ahead and at a public footpath sign turn right **B** up steps and walk along a narrow path between a wire fence on the left and a hedge on the right. Where the fence on the left ends, continue along the right-hand edge of a field. At the field corner the path continues ahead through woodland; it is narrow, overgrown and indistinct in places but there are white arrow-markers. Keep more or less in a straight line, later the path becomes more obvious. At a T-junction indicated by arrows on a tree trunk, turn sharp left, head gently uphill and, where arrows indicate the next path junction, turn right and continue uphill; the path curves left to reach a crossroads of paths. Turn sharp right, between a white-arrowed tree and a white-arrowed telegraph pole, to climb a stile and continue across a field to another one. Climb this and keep ahead over a third stile on to a lane.

Turn left along the lane for 200 yds (183m), and at a public footpath and bridleway sign turn right **C** through a metal gate to walk along the right-hand edge of a field, by trees and then by a wire fence on the right. Keep in a straight line

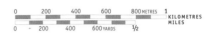

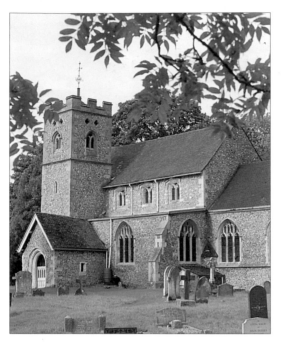

Great Hampden church

climb a stile and head gently downhill through mixed woodland to climb another stile at the far end. Continue straight across a field to climb a stile on to a road **E**. Cross the road and climb a stile opposite, at a public footpath sign. Take the path ahead through more woodland. At a crossroads of paths a white arrow directs you to the right to emerge into a field. Continue straight across the field heading towards a gap in the hedge at the far end.

Go through this gap, head uphill through a conifer wood, and on leaving the trees bear slightly left and walk across a field making for the trees on the far side. Here, at a white arrow on a tree, continue along a path, by a wire fence on the left – later the path becomes a drive – to a lane in the hamlet of Little Hampden. Turn right, heading downhill along the lane to the tiny, charming Little Hampden church, noted for its 15th-century timber-framed porch.

Opposite the church turn left **F**, at a public bridleway sign, along a track that heads downhill, meandering along the left-hand edge of a field, and then climbs up to the edge of woodland. Pass through a gap in the trees to head steeply uphill through the wood, keeping on the main path all the while; at the top you emerge from the trees and continue between wire fences to a metal gate. Go through the gate and keep ahead along a concrete path, by a hedge on the left, to a farm. Pass to the left of the farm buildings to reach a lane.

Turn left, here rejoining the outward route **A** and then turn right along a track to retrace your steps to the start. ●

along the right-hand edge of a series of fields, going through a succession of metal gates and finally continuing along the left-hand edge of woodland to a road. Bear left, keep ahead at a crossroads – in the direction of Great Hampden, Speen and Princes Risborough – and where the road bends sharply left, continue along a tarmac drive to pass between Hampden House on the right and Great Hampden church on the left. The most famous member of the Hampden family – lords of the manor – was John Hampden, a leading Parliamentary opponent of Charles I, whose refusal to pay ship money in 1641 helped to trigger off the Civil War. He was killed in 1643 while fighting for the Parliamentary army. Hampden House was almost totally rebuilt in the 18th century.

Where the tarmac drive turns right into the grounds of the house, keep ahead through a gate and immediately turn right over a stile **D**. Walk across a field, passing the front of Hampden House,

Petersham and Richmond Park

Start	Richmond, on east side of bridge
Distance	6½ miles (10.5km)
Approximate time	3½ hours
Parking	Richmond
Refreshments	Pubs, cafés and restaurants at Richmond, pub at Petersham, restaurant at Pembroke Lodge
Ordnance Survey maps	Landranger 176 (West London), Pathfinders 1174, TQ 07/17 (Staines, Heathrow Airport & Richmond) and 1175, TQ 27/37 (Wimbledon & Dulwich)

Richmond Park was first enclosed as a royal hunting park by Charles I in the 1630s and there has been public access since the 18th century. It remains a large tract (nearly 2500 acres/1013 ha) of surprisingly open and unchanged country on the edge of suburban west London, close to motorways and Heathrow Airport. The walk starts with an attractive stroll by the Thames and continues across meadows to the village of Petersham. Then there is an easy climb on to the ridge above the river, and the rest of the route is through the woodland and across the rough grassland of the park, still well stocked with deer. Towards the end there is the classic and still beautiful view over the winding Thames from Richmond Hill.

Until the late 15th century the area around Richmond was known as Sheene, but when Henry VII built a new palace there he renamed it Richmond after his earldom in Yorkshire. This palace, where Elizabeth I died in 1603, was demolished during the Cromwellian period and only part of the gateway and fragments of the walls remain, incorporated into the adjacent later houses. With its proximity to London and rural surroundings, Richmond has always been a desirable area and there are many handsome 17th- and 18th-century houses, especially around spacious Richmond Green.

The walk starts on the east side of Richmond Bridge. Facing the bridge turn left on to the wide tarmac path to follow an attractive stretch of the Thames and, after passing the Three Pigeons, continue across gardens, bearing slightly left away from the river.

At the end of the gardens **Ⓐ** keep ahead to cross another tarmac path, go through a metal kissing-gate and continue along the path ahead across Petersham Meadows. On reaching the far end pass through a metal barrier and walk along a hedge-lined path, then along a track, into Petersham, passing to the right of the church. On reaching the road turn left. Where the road curves left, opposite Dysarts pub, turn right **B** through a gate into Petersham Park. Almost immediately bear left off the tarmac path, at a sign to Pembroke Lodge, and follow a broad grassy path uphill across the parkland. At a fork keep to the wider, left-hand path and continue up to go through a metal gate at the top. Then turn right **C** along a well-defined path, passing flower beds and continuing through trees to reach Pembroke Lodge, an 18th-century hunting lodge which is now a restaurant.

Walk along the paved terrace in front of the lodge and continue along a tarmac path through an area of widely-spaced trees. Where the path curves left, keep ahead along a gravel path through bushes and go through a metal gate to enter Richmond Park. Continue ahead along the ridge – there are several paths here – keeping parallel to the road on the left and enjoying fine views to the right over the Thames Valley.

On reaching a crossroads and signpost at Ham Cross **D**, turn left, in the Isabella Plantation direction, along a park road. After about 50 yds (46m) turn half-right to follow a clear, broad, grassy path which leads to the parking area in front of the gate of Isabella Plantation. Go through the gate and follow the path ahead through this lovely wooded area of azaleas, rhododendrons and heathers. Pass to the left of a pond and continue by the left side of a small stream – there are lots of paths, but keep to the left of the stream all the time to go through another gate on the far side of the plantation **E**. Ahead is a broad gravel path and to the left are two grassy paths. Turn half-left to take the middle one of these three paths, that heads across the park between bracken, crosses a track and continues along the left edge of woodland, heading gently downhill. Where the edge of the woodland curves right, the path crosses another

track, bears slightly right and continues towards a park road, bearing right to a junction of roads at a signpost just to the right of a car park.

Cross the road and keep ahead along a rather faint grassy path that heads in a straight line towards the right-hand edge of Spankers Hill Wood. On reaching the edge of the wood you join a broad path, but after a short distance turn left **F**, by a wooden bench, to head uphill through the wood. There are several paths but keep in a straight line through the middle of the wood, later heading gently downhill. Near the bottom end look out for a small,

stagnant pond and pass to the left of it to emerge from the wood on to the edge of open grassland. Ahead is a narrow path that heads across the grass; on reaching the crest of a hill the walls of White Lodge are seen just to the right. This former hunting lodge, built for George II in 1727 and the birthplace of Edward VIII, now houses the Royal Ballet School.

Continue along the straight path across open grassland, crossing several more paths, to reach another park road. Cross the road, keep ahead to reach a second road, just in front of the fence of White Lodge, and bear left along it. At a T-junction turn right and about 50 yds (46m) ahead, in front of White Lodge, turn left **G** along Queen's Ride – a broad grassy ride lined by trees stretching ahead, that goes first gently downhill and then gradually uphill. Follow this ride for

A classic view of the Thames from Richmond

almost 1½ miles (2.4km), later keeping alongside a park road on the right, to leave the park at Richmond Gate **H**.

Keep ahead along Richmond Hill, passing in front of the Royal Star and Garter Home, and soon there is the classic and remarkably unchanged view from Queen's Terrace over the winding Thames, looking much as it did when Turner and other artists painted it. Continue to the end of the terrace, where there is a choice of routes back to the start. The most straightforward way is to continue along the road. An alternative way to return is to turn left through a gate into Terrace Gardens, head down steps and walk along one of the many paths through the colourful gardens down to a metal gate in the bottom right-hand corner, opposite the Three Pigeons. Go through the gate, cross the road, turn right and retrace your steps along the riverside path. ●

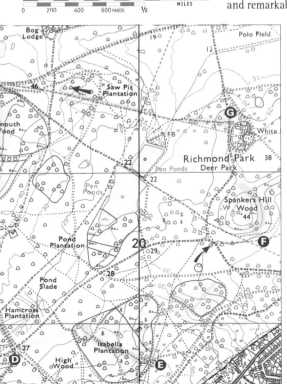

Henley-on-Thames and Hambleden

Henley-on-Thames and Hambleden

Start	Henley-on-Thames
Distance	7 miles (11.3km)
Approximate time	3½ hours
Parking	Henley-on-Thames
Refreshments	Pubs, restaurants and cafés at Henley-on-Thames, pub at Aston, pub at Hambleden
Ordnance Survey maps	Landranger 175 (Reading & Windsor), Explorer 3 (Chiltern Hills South)

The walk begins by crossing the Thames and heading up through Remenham Wood and across fields to the hamlet of Aston before descending to re-cross the river at Mill End. It then continues through a beautiful Chiltern valley to the picturesque and unspoilt village of Hambleden. From here the route climbs up through Ridge Wood, descends to the river again and follows an attractive riverside path back to Henley.

Since the 18th century Henley has been one of the most popular and fashionable of Thames-side towns. It stands on a beautiful stretch of the river, crossed by a dignified 18th-century bridge, and has a number of attractive Georgian and earlier buildings. The famous annual regatta was first held in 1839. The mainly 15th-century church, whose tower dominates most of the views from the river, is situated near the bridge at the bottom end of Hart Street where the walk begins.

Start by crossing Henley Bridge, turn left along Remenham Lane **A**, and at a public footpath sign turn right through a kissing-gate. Walk along a track that keeps close to the right-hand edge of a field, and where the track bends to the left, keep ahead to pass through a hedge gap, at a public footpath sign. Bear left to follow a faint but discernible path diagonally across a field to a public

footpath sign on the edge of trees in the far corner.

Head uphill through the trees, climb a stile and bear slightly left to continue along the top inside-edge of the sloping woodland. On leaving the trees bear right and head across grass, veering away from the fence on the left, to climb a stile. Continue along a narrow path through Remenham Wood, first ascending and then descending gently to emerge from the woodland on to a track. Cross it and take the path ahead across a field, from which there are fine views over the Thames Valley to the Chilterns, to reach a public footpath sign and a lane on the far side. Turn left along the lane and, at a public footpath sign, turn right **B** over a stile beside a metal gate and walk along a broad track across fields, later keeping by the right-hand edge of a belt of trees. Where the track turns left, continue

downhill along a narrow path by the left-hand edge of a field to a stile. Climb it and keep ahead down to a road **C**.

Turn left into the hamlet of Aston, turn left again at a junction by the Flower Pot Hotel, and at a public footpath sign turn right along a broad track **D**. Pass beside a metal gate and continue along this pleasant track as it winds across fields

down to the River Thames. Bear left to follow the river to Hambleden Lock, turn right through a gate to cross the lock and continue across a long metal footbridge above a weir to the attractive building of Hambleden Mill, which is now converted into apartments. Continue along a tarmac path between fences and then turn left between cottages to the road at Mill End.

Turn right, take the first turning on the left **E**, signposted to Hambleden, Skirmett and Fingest, and follow the road for ¼ mile (400m). At a junction for a minor road on the right to Rotten Row **F**, go through a gate, at public footpath and Circular Walk signs. Continue along the left-hand edge of a field, by a hedge on the left and keeping parallel with the road, through the lovely, gentle, wooded Hamble valley. Soon the cottages and church of Hambleden village are seen ahead. Go through a kissing-gate in the tapering far corner of a field, cross a track and climb a stile to continue across meadows bordering Hamble Brook on the right. At the far end of the meadows go through a metal kissing-gate on to a lane **G**. The village is to the right over the bridge. With its attractive brick-and-flint, red-tiled cottages, church, inn and manor house, Hambleden is the quintessential English village and one of the most delightful in the Chilterns. The mainly 14th-century church has undergone several alterations; the western tower was added in the 18th century and the whole building was restored during the Victorian era. In the churchyard is the grave of W.H. Smith, founder of the chain of booksellers, who lived at nearby Greenlands.

Approaching Hambleden village

The route continues to the left along the lane to the road. Cross the road and at a public footpath sign take the tarmac, hedge-lined path ahead, climbing steadily and later continuing through the attractive Ridge Wood. At a fork keep ahead, in the direction of a white arrow; as you climb there are some fine views through the trees on the left over the Hamble valley, and at the top a superb view ahead over the Thames Valley. The path now descends to a crossroad of paths. Turn first right and then immediately left; ahead is a gate on the edge of the woodland. Go through the gate, continue along the left-hand edge of a field, by a hedge and wire fence on the left, climb a stile and keep in the same direction across the next field to go through a kissing-gate on to a road **H**.

Turn right along the road – there is a footpath beside it – for ¼ mile (400m). At a public footpath sign turn left **J** over a stile to follow a rather indistinct but straight path across parkland, crossing in turn a tarmac drive and three footbridges before reaching the riverbank. Follow the Thames back to Henley, crossing a series of footbridges and passing first Temple Island to the left, Remenham church on the opposite bank of the river, and Fawley Court, the latter built in the late 17th century by Wren and situated at the end of a poplar-lined channel that gives it a Dutch air. Towards the end of this section there are fine views ahead of Henley's bridge and church tower.

At the end of the last meadow turn right through a metal kissing-gate, walk along the left-hand edge of a field, by hedges and a wire fence on the left, and continue along an enclosed and partially tree-lined path to go through a metal gate on to a road. Turn left into Henley, turn left again at a T-junction and keep ahead as far as the market place, just to the left of Henley Town Hall. Here turn left down Hart Street to return to the start. ●

Runnymede and Windsor Great Park

Start	Bishopsgate entrance to Windsor Great Park. Follow signs to Savill Gardens from A328 at Engelfield Green and turn along Bishopsgate Road
Distance	7 miles (11.3km)
Approximate time	3½ hours
Parking	Bishopsgate Road
Refreshments	Pub at Bishopsgate, pub at Engelfield Green, pub just before Savill Gardens, café at Savill Gardens entrance
Ordnance Survey maps	Landranger 176 (West London), Pathfinders 1173, SU87/97 (Windsor) and 1174, TQ 07/17 (Staines, Heathrow Airport & Richmond)

Historic interest is interwoven with riverside meadows, woodland and parkland on this varied walk. Runnymede is the site of one of the best-known events in English history, the signing of Magna Carta, and there is a memorial to the occasion there. Nearby is a memorial to President Kennedy, and the Commonwealth Air Forces Memorial is on Cooper's Hill above. Windsor Great Park was originally carved from Windsor Forest and its 3000 acres (1215 ha) are the main remnants of what was once a huge area of forest that stretched across much of Surrey and Berkshire. Towards the end of the walk is a memorable view from the Copper Horse, the equestrian statue of George III, looking down the Long Walk to the dramatic outline of Windsor Castle.

Start by walking away from the park entrance along Bishopsgate Road, passing the Fox and Hounds. Bear left along Crimp Hill, take the first turning on the right **Ⓐ**, Ridgemead Road, and where the road bends right, keep ahead across grass (cutting a corner) to turn left along the A328. At a public footpath sign turn right **Ⓑ** through a metal gate and walk along a tarmac, tree-lined track through grounds belonging to Brunel University. Keep ahead at a fork, pass beside a gate at a public footpath sign, and continue in a straight line – later the tarmac track becomes a rough track – heading downhill to reach the John F. Kennedy memorial. Continue past this, descending a series of steps through woods. Go through a gate on the edge of the trees and turn right **Ⓒ** on to a grassy path along the right-hand edge of Runnymede Meadows to the Magna Carta Memorial, a gift of the American Bar Association, accessible via a gate on the right. It commemorates the signing in these meadows of Magna Carta by a reluctant King John in 1215.

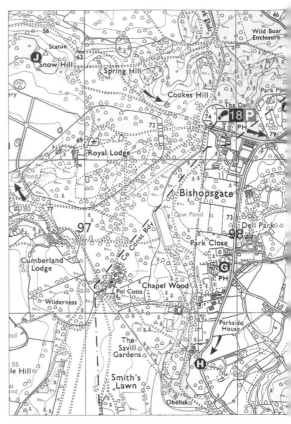

At the memorial turn left along a straight path across the meadow, by a wire fence on the right, and cross the A308 to the Thames opposite Magna Carta Island. Turn right along the river, but after about ¼ mile (400m) look out for a public footpath sign and stile on the other side of the main road and turn right **D** away from the river to re-cross the road and climb this stile. Walk along a straight path across the meadow once more – ahead is the Commonwealth Air Forces Memorial on the wooded slopes of Cooper's Hill. Go through a metal kissing-gate on the far side of the meadow and keep ahead along a narrow path, between a wire fence on the right and a line of trees on the left, to climb a waymarked stile ahead. Continue up steps through some attractive woodland; the path bends first to the left and then curves right to a metal kissing-gate. Go through the gate, turn right along a tarmac drive and a short distance ahead the drive bears right to the Commonwealth Air Forces Memorial. This impressive and dignified monument to the airmen who died in World War II stands in immaculate grounds and commands fine views over the Thames Valley.

At the point where the drive bears right, go left through a metal kissing-gate, at a public footpath sign, and walk along a tarmac path by the left-hand edge of a sports field. The path later runs between walls and fences, turning first right and then left and continues as a rough, enclosed path to a road. Cross the road, go through the metal barrier opposite and continue along an enclosed tarmac path to pass through another metal barrier on to a road **E**. Turn right, and at a junction just ahead bear left along Barley Mow Road to a crossroads. Cross over, continue along the left side of Engelfield Green, passing a pub. At a fork keep left along Northcroft Road, following the road around a left- and a right-hand bend. At the next left bend keep ahead over a stile **F**, at a public footpath sign, on to a path that keeps along the left edge of rough grassland, by hedges and fences bordering gardens on the left.

Pass through a fence gap, at a yellow waymark, and continue across the corner of a field to climb a stile. Keep ahead to turn left through another fence gap and continue along a faint path that heads diagonally across a field to pass through another fence gap in the field corner. Bear right along the right-hand edge of a field, by a hedge and fence on the right, and follow the field-edge around to the left.

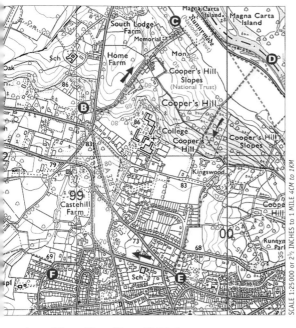

SCALE 1:25 000 or 2½ INCHES to 1 MILE 4CM to 1KM

```
0    200   400   600   800 METRES   1
                                       KILOMETRES
                                       MILES
0    200   400   600 YARDS   ½
```

Cumberland Gate in front. At a road junction in front of the lodge, turn right through a gate and then turn left to continue in the same direction as before along a path through trees, by a fence on the left. On reaching a tarmac drive turn left along it towards Cumberland Lodge, then bear right along a track, passing to the right of a tennis court and continuing to a road junction.

Turn left, and then turn right along a track that heads downhill through trees, by a fence on the right, passing to the right of Ox Pond to emerge into a more open landscape. Continue along the broad, hedge-lined, grass ride towards the Copper Horse statue straight ahead. Over to the right Royal Lodge can be seen. Go through a metal gate in a deer fence and keep ahead to the huge, equestrian statue of George III erected in 1831 on Snow Hill. This is the highest point in the park and a magnificent viewpoint over the woods and lawns of the park, the Thames Valley and especially along the impressive 3-mile (4.8km) avenue of the Long Walk, created by Charles II in 1680, to the profile of Windsor Castle on the skyline.

In front of the statue ❶ turn right along a grassy track into woodland, bear left on meeting another track and continue straight ahead along a grassy ride to the right of a bridge and the road below. From here there are more fine views of Windsor Castle.

On meeting the road turn right alongside it, go through a metal gate in the deer fence again and bear left along a tree-lined path to rejoin the road in front of the Bishopsgate entrance. Go through the gate to return to the start. ●

Go down steps and continue along a narrow path, enclosed by a hedge and trees on the left and iron railings on the right, to emerge on to a track. Keep ahead along the track, passing in front of a row of houses, to a road just to the right of the Sun pub ❻. Bear left along Wick Lane, passing in front of the pub, for just over ¼ mile (400m) to reach the entrance to Savill Gardens ❼, a colourful 35-acre garden begun in 1932, well worth a visit.

Turn right across the car park, in the direction signposted 'Obelisk Monument and Pond', and go through a gate in the far corner to enter Windsor Great Park. Bear right and cross a tarmac drive to the obelisk that commemorates the Duke of Cumberland, son of George II and victor of Culloden. In front of the obelisk turn right along a track which passes to the right of the Obelisk Pond and crosses a bridge over the end of it. Keep ahead along a broad grassy ride, between the boundary of Savill Gardens on the right and the open expanse of Smith's Lawn on the left, making for the brick lodge of

Northchurch and Berkhamsted Commons

Start	Berkhamsted
Distance	7 miles (11.3km)
Approximate time	3½ hours
Parking	Berkhamsted
Refreshments	Pubs and cafés at Berkhamsted
Ordnance Survey maps	Landranger 165 (Aylesbury & Leighton Buzzard), Explorer 2 (Chiltern Hills North)

Occupying the main ridge of the Chilterns to the north of Berkhamsted is an area of woodland and open grassy commons, much of which forms part of the National Trust's vast Ashridge Estate. After a short stroll along the towpath of the Grand Union Canal, the route climbs out of the valley and continues across this common land, where there are fine views from the more open sections. Apart from the short and easy climb on to the ridge near the start and the final descent back into Berkhamsted, this is a relatively flat and undemanding walk.

Berkhamsted lies in a valley that has always been a major routeway through the Chilterns from London to the midlands and north – the Grand Union Canal, a busy railway line and a main road pass through it. The Normans recognised Berkhamsted's strategic importance and built the castle; much of the later stonework of this once important fortress and royal residence has vanished to reveal the 11th-century earthworks of the original, simple motte and bailey construction. Berkhamsted also has a large 13th-century church and, despite much modern development, retains some attractive old cottages.

Begin by the 19th-century former town hall, now an arcade of small shops, and turn down Lower Kings Road, in the direction of the castle. Just before reaching the canal bridge go down steps and turn left along the towpath of the Grand Union Canal Ⓐ. Pass under two footbridges, go past a lock and at the next bridge turn left to a road. Turn sharply right Ⓑ to cross first the canal bridge and then a railway bridge and continue to a road junction.

Turn right on to Bridgewater Road but almost immediately turn left to head uphill through new housing along the appropriately named Bridle Way. At a T-junction cross the road and keep ahead Ⓒ, at a bridleway sign, along a path between hedges and scrub and then through woodland. The path bears right to emerge from the trees on to a tarmac drive. Continue along the track straight ahead and where it turns right to a house, keep ahead along a path through more woodland to reach a tarmac drive in front of Northchurch Farm. Cross the drive,

SCALE 1:26316 or about 2½ INCHES to 1 MILE 3.8CM to 1KM

0 200 400 600 800 METRES 1
0 200 400 600 YARDS ½
KILOMETRES
MILES

continue along a narrow path that winds between trees and bracken, and on reaching a T-junction turn right along a more clearly defined path. Keep ahead, ignoring all side paths, and at the next T-junction bear right to reach a road **D**.

Cross the road and continue along a path between trees and bracken. Go across two tracks and soon after crossing the second one bear left, at a blue waymark, to keep along the left-hand edge of the open grassland of Northchurch Common. The path curves slightly left to reach a path junction on the edge of woodland **E**, where you bear slightly right at a bridleway sign into the trees – not fully right along the edge of the common.

On emerging from the trees continue along the left-hand edge of open common again, and at a fork take the left-hand path to re-enter woodland. At a path junction, indicated by a blue-waymarked post, turn right to continue through some more superb woodland to emerge on to a road **F**.

Turn right to a T-junction, cross the road and continue along a grassy track opposite, through the woodland of Berkhamsted Common, following bridleway signs. Pass to the left of an abandoned farm, after which the route continues along a clearer, stony, well-surfaced track. Keep to the left of Coldharbour Farm, and at a crossroads of tracks continue straight ahead. Where the track forks, take the right-hand track, then continue along the left inside-edge of woodland, with grand views across open common to the left, to reach a track and bridleway sign on the edge of the next belt of woodland. Cross the track and keep straight ahead through the woodland to reach a small, open, grassy area where

Berkhamsted Castle

there is a crossroads of paths **G**. This can be a little difficult to spot as there are no waymarks to act as a guide.

Here turn right and after about 100 yds (91m), where the path bears left, look out for a narrower but reasonably clear path that leads off to the right. Follow this path downhill through trees to a stile on the edge of the woodland. Climb the stile and continue along the left-hand edge of a field, by a wire fence and hedge on the left, to join a track. Go through a metal gate, walk along the track, climb a stile to the right of a farm and continue along the right-hand edge of a succession of fields and over a series of stiles, by a hedge and wire fence on the right all the time. Finally walk along a path between sports fields and continue along a tarmac drive and on through a car park to a road.

Keep ahead along the road, passing to the right of Berkhamsted Castle, pass under a railway bridge and turn right in front of the station. The road bends left to cross the Grand Union Canal and return to the starting point. ●

Marlow and Hurley

Start	Marlow
Distance	7 miles (11.3km). Shorter version 4½ miles (7.2km)
Approximate time	3½ hours (2½ hours for shorter version)
Parking	Marlow
Refreshments	Pubs and cafés at Marlow, pub at Hurley, light refreshments at Temple Lock, pub on A4155
Ordnance Survey maps	Landranger 175 (Reading & Windsor), Explorer 3 (Chiltern Hills South)

A steady climb out of Marlow is followed by a gradual descent through the peaceful 'Happy Valley' and a stroll along a tree-lined track and across fields to reach the banks of the Thames. At this point the shorter version follows the riverside path directly back to Marlow, but the full walk crosses the river via the Temple Footbridge to make a detour to the village of Hurley. The last 1½ miles (2.4km) of the route is along an outstandingly beautiful part of the Thames from Temple Lock to Marlow.

The spacious riverside town of Marlow is situated close to some of the most attractive stretches of the Thames. Views of the town are dominated by the suspension bridge over the river and by the church, both dating from the 19th century, and the town as a whole has a pleasantly old-fashioned Victorian atmosphere.

Start at the north end of the suspension bridge by the church. Walk away from the bridge and turn first left into Pound Lane. Opposite a car park turn right along a wide tarmac path between walls to a road, turn right and then turn left along Oxford Road. Just past the Crown and Anchor turn left **Ⓐ**, at a public footpath sign, along an enclosed tarmac path. Follow it around right and left bends, heading gently uphill and finally around another right-hand bend to reach a road.

Cross the road, keep ahead along another uphill enclosed path, crossing one road and at the second one, Ryans Mount, turning left to the end of the road. Here pass through a metal barrier and immediately turn right along a broad tarmac path which heads gently uphill through a modern housing area. Cross a road at the top and keep ahead across grass to a public footpath sign to the left of a school entrance. Climb a stile and continue along an enclosed path, following it around a sharp left bend and bearing right to a stile. Climb the stile, then bear left along a tarmac path, follow it around a right-hand bend and turn left to a road. Continue along the road, turn right at a T-junction along Spinfield Lane, and opposite Bovingdon Heights turn left, at a public footpath sign, on to a track.

The track bends first right and then left to reach a stile beside a metal gate. Climb the stile and keep ahead along the left-hand edge of a field. Climb another stile and continue along a path which now

SCALE 1:25000 or 2½ INCHES to 1 MILE 4CM to 1KM

| 0 | 200 | 400 | 600 | 800 METRES | 1 |
| 0 | 200 | 400 | 600 YARDS | | ½ |

KILOMETRES
MILES

descends, by a wire fence on the right, into a valley. Just before reaching the next stile in the field corner, turn sharp left **B** to follow a grassy path through this valley, nicknamed Happy Valley, with grand views ahead looking across the Thames Valley. Later the path keeps by a line of trees on the right to a stile. Climb it and keep ahead, by a hedge on the right, to reach a metal kissing-gate by farm buildings. Go through the gate and turn left along a tarmac drive to a road. Turn right, and where the road bends to the right by the Hare and Hounds, bear left **C**

along a tarmac drive signposted 'Private Road To Low Grounds Farm'.

Go through a white kissing-gate and continue along a straight drive for ½ mile (800m); this is pleasantly tree-lined at first, then emerges from the trees to give fine views to the left. At East Lodge follow the drive as it turns left **D**, pass to the left of Low Grounds Farm and continue along the track as it bends first to the right and then to the left and crosses fields to reach the river **E**.

For the shorter version of the walk, turn left here to return to Marlow.

For the full walk, turn right and follow the Thames past Temple Lock and up to Temple Footbridge, opened in 1989 on the site of the former Temple Ferry. Turn left over the bridge and turn right to continue along a shady path on the south bank of the river. Pass through a gate at the corner of woodland, continue across meadows and turn right over a footbridge on to Hurley Lock Island. Turn left, walk past the lock, turn left over a similar footbridge, descend steps and follow a tarmac path into the peaceful village of Hurley. The Norman church originally belonged to a small priory and there are a few monastic remains, including a dovecote and tithe barn.

Continue along a road through the village and, just in front of Ye Olde Bell Inn, turn left **F**, at a public footpath sign, through a metal kissing-gate to continue along a shady, fence-enclosed path. Cross a track and keep ahead by some fencing

bordering a caravan site on the left. Climb a stile and continue along a broad track. Where the track bends to the right turn left **G** over a stile, at a public footpath sign, to walk along a pleasant, tree-lined path which leads back to the river. Turn right to retrace your steps over Temple Footbridge to the point where you first joined the river **E**.

Follow the riverside path for nearly $1^{1}/_{2}$ miles (2.4km) back to Marlow, a delightful finale to the walk. Looking over the fields to the left, the Chilterns can be seen and across the river are views of the buildings of Bisham Abbey, a Tudor house on the site of a medieval monastery which is now owned by the Sports Council, and the beautiful 12th-century Bisham church. Towards the end there are equally fine views ahead of Marlow. By the bridge the riverside path turns left and heads up to the road at the starting point.　●

The 12th-century church at Bisham

Aldbury, Ivinghoe Beacon and Ashridge

Aldbury, Ivinghoe Beacon and Ashridge

Start	Aldbury
Distance	7 miles (11.3km)
Approximate time	3½ hours
Parking	Aldbury - alternatively, Pitstone Hill or Bridgewater Monument
Refreshments	Pubs at Aldbury, tearoom at Bridgewater Monument (summer weekends only)
Ordnance Survey maps	Landranger 165 (Aylesbury & Leighton Buzzard), Explorer 2 (Chiltern Hills North)

This outstanding walk starts in a picturesque village, proceeds along the Chiltern escarpment to Ivinghoe Beacon – one of the highest viewpoints in the Chilterns – and returns through part of the magnificent woodlands of the National Trust's Ashridge Estate. There are several climbs but the paths are good, the route easy to follow, and the views superb all the way.

All the ingredients that make up the classic English village scene are present in Aldbury: charming brick and half-timbered cottages (some thatched) and a pub grouped around a triangular green; duck pond, stocks and whipping-post standing on the green; and a short distance away a medieval church. To enhance the scene still further, the village is set against the glorious backdrop of the beech woods of Ashridge. It is not surprising that Aldbury has frequently been used as a film set.

Start by walking along the road in the Tring direction, passing the church, and at a public footpath sign to Pitstone Hill turn right over a stile **Ⓐ**. Head across to climb another stile to the left of a metal gate, continue along the left-hand edge of a field, by farm buildings on the left, but before reaching the end of the buildings look out for and climb a stile on the left.

Immediately turn right along a narrow enclosed path, climb a stile, keep ahead to climb another and continue along a path between wire fences.

Climb two stiles in quick succession and continue across part of a golf-course, following a fairly obvious grassy path and keeping in the same direction as before – a series of yellow-waymarked posts aid route-finding. Later, keep along the left edge of trees and a hedge to go through a kissing-gate in the top right-hand corner of a field, and continue between trees, bushes and scrub to a fingerpost at a path junction. Bear left and then turn right up a flight of steps, here joining the Ridgeway.

Follow the acorn-symbol Ridgeway waymarks over Pitstone Hill. Initially the route passes through woodland, but after

0	200	400	600	800 METRES	1	
						KILOMETRES
						MILES
0	200	400	600 YARDS	½		

SCALE 1:25000 or 2½ INCHES to 1 MILE 4CM to 1KM

climbing a stile, it continues over open downland with some fine views to the left over the Vale of Aylesbury, even though the dominant feature is Pitstone Cement Works. The path later descends and curves gradually to the right, keeping close to a wire fence on the right, finally bearing left to a stile in front of Pitstone Hill car park. On this descent the escarpment and next part of the route can be seen stretching ahead to Ivinghoe Beacon.

Climb the stile, pass through the car park **B**, cross a lane and take the path opposite that heads straight across a large field. Climb another stile and continue across the next field. The path then keeps below a bank on the right, ascending and curving left to a stile. Do not climb it but pass to the left of it and head across, keeping parallel to a hedge and wire fence on the right, to a Ridgeway marker post on the edge of woodland. Continue through the trees and on emerging from them keep ahead downhill, by a wire fence on the right. Turn right over a stile in the fence, head uphill through an area of scrub and bushes, and then continue downhill to climb a stile. Bear left down to the corner of a road **C**. Cross the road and follow the left-hand one of the two tracks ahead up to the summit of Ivinghoe Beacon, marked by a triangulation pillar **D**. This outlying spur of the Chiltern range, 764ft (233m) high, gives a magnificent panorama over the Vale of Aylesbury, along the Chiltern escarpment

Looking towards Ivinghoe Beacon

from Dunstable Downs to Coombe Hill and across to the slopes of Ashridge Park.

Retrace your steps to the road **C**, cross over and then turn left, at a National Trust marker post, along a pleasant path that initially keeps parallel to the road on the left, heading uphill between trees to join a track. Bear left along the track, which curves left to reach an open grassy area beside the road. Turn right alongside hedges on the right, parallel to the road, and at the end of this grassy area turn right **E** along a track signposted 'Private Drive to Clipper Down Cottage and permitted footpath and bridleway to Bridgewater Monument'.

Almost the whole of the remainder of the walk is through part of the splendid beech woods of the Ashridge Estate, over 4000 acres (1620 ha) of open grassland, commons and woodlands belonging to the National Trust. Follow the track through this attractive woodland, taking care to keep on the main track all the while, to Clipper Down Cottage. Go through a gate, at a Bridgewater Monument sign, pass to the right of the cottage and continue along another track: at intervals there are superb views to the right from these wooded slopes across the flatter country of the vale. Pass to the left of a log cabin and soon after crossing a footbridge you reach the Bridgewater Monument **F**, erected in 1832 in memory of the third Duke of Bridgewater, the great canal-builder and owner of Ashridge. The view from the top is well worth the climb.

Keep ahead past the monument to join a track in front of the National Trust shop, information centre and tearoom. Turn right and follow the track downhill through woodland; a gap on the right reveals a superb view of Aldbury village and church nestling in the valley below. At a fork take the right-hand lower track to continue downhill to a road and turn right for a short distance to return to the centre of Aldbury village. ●

Ibstone, Turville and Fingest

Start	Ibstone Common
Distance	8 miles (12.9km)
Approximate time	4 hours
Parking	Roadside parking beside Ibstone Common near Fox Country Hotel and Restaurant
Refreshments	Restaurant at Ibstone, pub at Turville, pub at Fingest
Ordnance Survey maps	Landranger 175 (Reading & Windsor), Explorer 3 (Chiltern Hills South)

There is a tranquillity and sense of remoteness about this walk which could place it in the more inaccessible parts of the Pennines or the depths of Dartmoor, but the landscape of beech woods and sweeping dry chalk valleys is unmistakably that of the Chilterns. The feeling of remoteness is further reinforced by the two villages that are passed through en route: *both Turville and Fingest are small, largely unchanged and apparently timeless villages with distinctive and interesting churches, tucked away in a quiet valley.*

The walk starts just to the south of the Fox Country Hotel and Restaurant, where you take a grassy path along the edge of Ibstone Common, by trees on the right, ignoring the public footpath sign here that directs you into the trees. On the far side turn left **Ⓐ** to continue along the edge of the rough open common, cross a drive, keep ahead through trees and continue along a stony, hedge-lined track, passing to the left of a cottage and heading downhill to a tarmac drive.

Turn right along the drive, and on entering trees bear left on to a path, at public footpath and bridleway signs, which briefly rejoins the track and then continues downhill through a narrow belt of woodland. Follow this descending tree-enclosed path all the while, and on reaching the bottom keep ahead. Where the path curves left, turn right on to a wide, clear path through trees to reach a lane about 50 yds (46m) ahead at a public footpath sign **Ⓑ**. Climb the stile opposite and head uphill across a field, by a wire fence on the right. All around are fine views over this lovely Chiltern valley. Climb a stile in the top corner of the field, bear slightly right to continue more steeply uphill through woodland, and just past a white arrow on a tree trunk, turn left on to a narrow but discernible flinty path through Idlecombe Wood.

The path, rough and sometimes overgrown at first, later broadens out and continues through beautiful beech woodland to a T-junction, where you turn right along a track which heads gently uphill to reach the top edge of woodland just in front of a barn and tarmac drive. Here turn left **Ⓒ** through a gate and follow a straight grassy path across a field, passing to the left of Turville Court. Go through a gate, continue – with a

SCALE 1:25 000 or 2½ INCHES to 1 MILE 4CM to 1KM

```
0     200    400    600    800 METRES   1
                                          KILOMETRES
                                          MILES
0     200    400    600 YARDS   ½
```

lovely view over the valley ahead – and at
the end of the field you start to descend,
initially along the right-hand edge of
woodland. Where the edge of the field
curves left, keep straight ahead downhill
across the field – a white arrow on a
telegraph pole points the way –
descending into the valley. At the bottom
bear left along an enclosed path and

continue down a road to a T-junction **D**
in the centre of Turville village, an idyllic
scene of old brick and half-timbered
cottages grouped around a green, pub and
restored late medieval church.

At the T-junction take the path opposite
between cottages; a disused windmill,
now a private residence, is on the top of
the hill directly in front. Do not climb the
stile immediately ahead but turn right
through a gate and head across a garden
to go through another gate. Turn right

and immediately bear left to head uphill across the corner of a field to a stile. Climb it, walk along a narrow path through a belt of trees to climb another stile on to a lane, cross the lane and continue along the path opposite. At a path junction bear right and, with a lovely view of the tower of Fingest church, head downhill to climb a stile on to a road on the edge of the village. Like Turville, Fingest has a picturesque collection of brick-and-timber houses, pub and church, but is even smaller. The church is one of the most unusual and interesting village churches in the Chilterns, noted for its plain, massive, twin-gabled Norman tower that looks out of proportion to the rest of the building.

Turn left into the village, passing to the right of the church. In front of the Chequers Inn turn left along Chequers Lane **E**. After ½ mile (800m) at a right-hand curve, go through a fence gap **F**, at public bridleway and footpath signs, and take the clear, wide path straight ahead. At a fork about 50 yds (46m) ahead, take the right-hand narrower path through a narrow belt of trees. Go through a gate to

Turville, deep in a fold of the Chilterns

emerge from the trees, continue along the right-hand edge of a field, by a hedge on the right, but look out for where the path bears slightly right to continue, between a hedge on the left and a wire fence on the right, to a gate.

Go through the gate, walk along the right-hand edge of a field, by a wire fence on the right, and then continue along the right edge of a belt of woodland, bearing right on meeting a track. After climbing a stile, go through a broader, mainly coniferous wooded area, to reach a crossroads of tracks. Keep straight ahead through woodland, keep ahead again at another path junction, and continue along the bottom edge of Penley Wood.

Look out for white arrows on a tree trunk, and a little further on there is a fork **G**. Take the left-hand grassy path – not very clear at first, but another white arrow acts as a useful guide – soon emerging from the trees to continue along the left-hand edge of a field. At the end of the field cross a track, keep ahead steadily uphill through more trees, and on leaving this final area of woodland you join a farm track. Ahead are the houses of Ibstone. Follow the track to a road and turn right to return to the start. ●

Coombe Hill and Chequers

Start	Wendover
Distance	8 miles (12.9km)
Approximate time	4½ hours
Parking	Wendover village centre. Alternatively, use railway station passed just after start
Refreshments	Pubs and cafés at Wendover
Ordnance Survey maps	Landranger 165 (Aylesbury & Leighton Buzzard), Explorer 2 (Chiltern Hills North)

This is one of the great walks of the Chilterns. From Wendover there is a long and steady climb to the summit of Coombe Hill, the highest and one of the most magnificent viewpoints in the Chilterns (the highest point is actually in Wendover Woods a short distance away). The route then drops down the steep face of the escarpment and continues across fields to the village of Ellesborough, whose church tower is visible from Coombe Hill. The rest of the walk follows an undulating route, punctuated by delightful woodland and passes Chequers, the Prime Minister's country residence, before the final descent into Wendover. There are a number of climbs but they are all gradual; in fact the steepest part of the walk is the descent from Coombe Hill.

The village of Wendover lies in an attractive position below the Chiltern escarpment and possesses some fine old cottages and Georgian houses; the church lies over ¼ mile (400m) to the south of the village centre.

Start at the bottom of the main street by the 19th-century clock tower, walk up the street and at the roundabout keep ahead, in the Ellesborough and Princes Risborough direction. Cross a railway bridge, continue uphill along the road for ¼ mile (400m) and at a right-hand bend bear left, at public bridleway and Ridgeway signs, on to a path **A**.

At a Bacombe Hill notice the path forks; continue along the right-hand path, signposted Ridgeway, and at the next fork continue along the left-hand path to head

up a series of steps. The well-defined path continues steadily uphill, sometimes between trees and bushes and at other times across open grassy areas, finally going through a kissing-gate and on to the Boer War monument on the summit of Coombe Hill **B**. From here, at 852ft (260m) the highest viewpoint in the Chilterns, a magnificent panorama unfolds over the Vale of Aylesbury, with Ellesborough church below. In clear weather the line of the Cotswolds is visible ahead, and to the right the Chiltern escarpment can be seen stretching away to Ivinghoe Beacon. This area was presented to the National Trust in 1918.

After passing the monument turn left, at a Ridgeway waymarked post with an acorn symbol, keeping just below the top

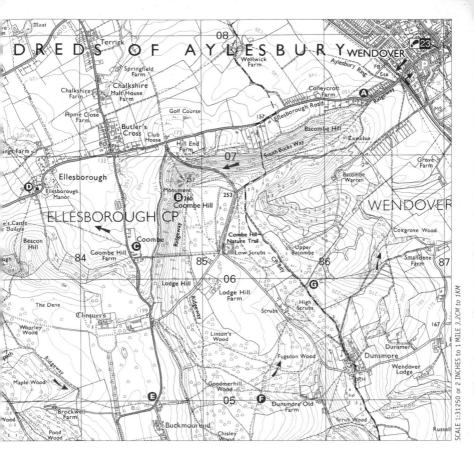

SCALE 1:31250 or 2 INCHES to 1 MILE 3.2CM to 1KM

```
0    200   400   600   800 METRES 1
                              KILOMETRES
                              MILES
0    200   400   600 YARDS   1/2
```

of the escarpment and enjoying superb views to the right. About 50 yds (46m) before reaching woodland in front and at the point where the Ridgeway starts to bear left at a waymarked post, bear right along a fainter and narrower grassy path to a stile in the trees. Do not climb the stile but turn right and head steeply downhill to the bottom of the escarpment, by a wire fence on the left, to a crossroads of paths. The flat-topped hill ahead is Beacon Hill, climbed later on the walk. At the crossroads keep ahead to go through a gate and continue along an enclosed track to a road by Coombe Hill Farm. Turn right, and at a public footpath sign turn left **C** to follow a clear path across a large field, later continuing along its right-hand edge, by a hedge on the right.

Pass through a fence in the field corner and turn right along a hedge-lined track to a road opposite Ellesborough's imposing medieval church.

Turn left along a path above the road and then turn left **D** over a stile, at a public footpath sign, and take a path that heads diagonally and gently uphill across a field to a stile. Climb it and continue in the same direction along a rather indistinct path over the shoulder of Beacon Hill, later picking up a clear path which bears slightly left and continues above woodland on the right to a stile on the edge of Ellesborough Warren. Climb the stile, continue through the wood, go up a flight of steps, and at the top you emerge from the trees and continue across a field to the next belt of woodland. The path enters Whorley Wood and crosses a tarmac track to a stile. Climb it, keep ahead along the left-hand edge of a field,

The Vale of Aylesbury from Coombe Hill

by a wire fence bordering woodland on the left, and where the trees on the left end, the path bears slightly right to a stile.

Climb the stile to rejoin the Ridgeway and continue along the left-hand edge of Maple Wood. Over to the left is Chequers, a large 16th-century house given to the nation in 1917 by Lord Lee of Fareham, to be used as a country retreat for Prime Ministers. The views from here across the valley to the wooded slopes on the other side are very pleasant. At a Ridgeway sign turn left over a stile, walk across a field, climb a stile, keep ahead to climb another and cross the main drive of Chequers – Victory Drive, a beech-lined avenue planted under the instructions of Winston Churchill in the 1960s. Climb a stile and follow the path ahead to climb another stile on to a road ❺. Cross the road and bear slightly left along the track opposite, at public bridleway and Ridgeway signs. At a fork follow the direction of a blue waymark and acorn symbol on a tree to take the right-hand track, which heads uphill to a junction of tracks and paths on the edge of Goodmerhill Wood.

Continue uphill through this beautiful woodland and, at the top, where the Ridgeway turns left, keep ahead to reach another crossroads of paths ❻. Turn left along a gently ascending path, then turn

right over a stile in a wire fence and continue in the same direction as before – there are plenty of yellow arrows on trees – to climb another stile. Keep ahead through Fugsdon Wood, climb a stile and continue downhill to climb another stile on to a lane.

Cross the lane, climb the stile opposite and continue through woodland to a T-junction of paths where you turn left. Keeping a sharp look-out for yellow arrows, follow a path that later bends right and continues through an area of young trees to a stile at a crossroads of paths ❼. Climb the stile, turn right, climb another stile and continue along a track between wire fences, past a junction of paths, until after about ¼ mile (400m) you reach a point where another path enclosed by wire fences forks off sharply on the left (almost doubling back). Take this path, which after a while enters Coxgrove Wood and bears right, heading gently downhill. Where an arrow on a tree indicates a fork, take the left-hand path to continue downhill through the wood, by a metal fence on the left.

Just after the fence ends, bear left – following the direction of a white arrow – to head uphill through the last of the many areas of beautiful woodland on this walk and continue to a stile on the edge of the wood. There is a fine open view ahead, looking towards Wendover. Climb the stile, bear slightly left to head downhill across a field, climb a stile on the far side and continue uphill along a grassy path, later between bushes, to climb another stile. Walk along a fence-lined path and, where the fences end, continue across a narrow grassy area between hedges, bearing left to a lane.

Turn right, and at a public footpath sign turn left over a stile and bear slightly right to walk across a field, heading down to a stile near the field corner. Climb this, continue down an enclosed path to a road and turn right to return to Wendover. ●

Chesham and Little Missenden

Start	Chesham
Distance	9 miles (14.5km)
Approximate time	4½ hours
Parking	Chesham
Refreshments	Pubs and cafés at Chesham, pubs at Little Missenden
Ordnance Survey maps	Landranger 165 (Aylesbury & Leighton Buzzard), Explorers 2 (Chiltern Hills North) and 3 (Chiltern Hills South)

From Chesham the route proceeds through a quiet, undulating and off-the-beaten-track landscape of rolling hills, dry valleys and woodland in the heart of the Chilterns. The halfway point is Little Missenden, a delightful village with an interesting church in the Misbourne valley. This is a long walk with some narrow and possibly overgrown paths between Little Missenden and Hyde Heath and plenty of ups and downs, but none of the uphill stretches are steep or lengthy.

Although much of the historic interest of Chesham, a traditional Chilterns furniture-making town, has disappeared through the process of modern redevelopment, there are still some handsome old buildings and attractive streets near the restored medieval church. The former town hall building was demolished in 1965 but part of it has recently been re-erected as a clock tower and makes a striking feature in the pedestrianised High Street.

Start by facing the war memorial in the centre of Chesham, turn left to a roundabout and cross the road to enter a park. After a short distance turn left along a broad, straight, tarmac path above Scottowe's Pond on the left, towards the church. In front of the churchyard entrance turn right **A**, at a public footpath sign, along a tarmac drive, later bearing slightly left off it to continue along a track into a field.

Keep along the left-hand edge of the field, beside trees on the left, and at the end of the field the path continues through trees to a stile. Climb it, keep ahead to climb over another stile – this part of the walk follows Chiltern Link waymarks – bear slightly left and head gently downhill across a field to go through a kissing-gate on to a lane. Cross this lane, climb the stile opposite and walk diagonally across a field to another stile. Climb over it and continue across the next field to climb a stile on to a lane. Turn right and, carefully following the Chiltern Link waymarks, ignore the first public bridleway sign to the left but at the second one, signposted to Herberts Hole and South Heath, turn left to climb over a stile on to a track **B**.

Follow the track through the dry valley bottom of Herberts Hole, a section of the walk that has a decidedly remote feel. At the point where the track ends, go through a metal gate, keep ahead to go through another gate and continue, by a hedge and wire fence on the right, to a third one. Go through the gate, continue along a track, between woodland on the left and a hedge on the right, and about 50 yds (46m) further on, look out for a yellow waymark where you turn left into the woodland **C**. Follow an uphill path through the trees which bends to the right, then climb a stile on the edge of the wood on to a lane.

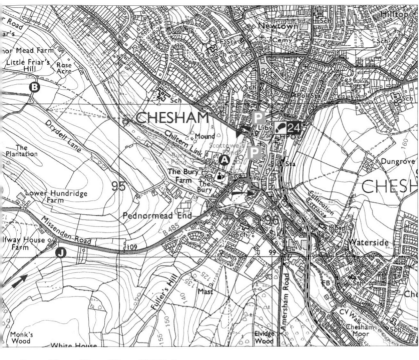

| 0 | 200 | 400 | 600 | 800 METRES | 1 |
| 0 | 200 | 400 | 600 YARDS | ½ | KILOMETRES MILES |

Turn left along the lane, ignore the first public footpath sign on the right to Reddings Farm, but at the second (half-hidden in a hedge and opposite a house), turn right **D** over a stile. Walk along the right-hand edge of fields, by a hedge and then a fence on the right, and where the fence ends keep ahead towards woodland. Go through a gap in the trees, but do not enter the next field. Instead bear slightly right on to a path that keeps along the left inside-edge of some attractive woodland – several white arrows point the way – to a T-junction of paths. Turn left to continue along the right inside-edge of the wood, go through a metal gate and, following the direction of a Circular Walk waymark, turn right along a tarmac drive between houses. At a yellow waymark turn left **E** along a hedge-lined path, passing to the right of a bungalow, climb a stile and continue along the left-hand edge of a field, by trees and a wire fence on the left. Climb another stile, keep along the right-

hand edge of the next field, by a wire fence on the right, to climb a wooden fence in the field corner. Bear slightly left to cross the next field – there is no visible path – and climb a stile on to a road.

Turn left, and at public footpath and Circular Walk signs turn right along a tarmac drive to The Hyde, passing to the left of a lodge. Where the drive turns right, bear slightly left to continue along a narrow path between trees and hedges to a stile. Climb it, continue along the right-hand edge of a field, by a fence on the right, climb another stile and keep in the same direction across the next field, heading down into a dip, then up again and bearing slightly right to climb a stile in the top right-hand corner. Cross a track and take the path ahead to enter woodland. The path – not very clearly defined – meanders along the left inside-edge of the wood. Look out for where it turns left through a gap in a hedge into a field.

Turn right along the right-hand edge of the field and then, just before the field-edge bends right, turn half-left to follow a grassy path across the field. On the other side turn right to continue along the edge of Mantle's Wood on the left, heading downhill. Ahead is a lovely view over a typical rolling Chilterns landscape. At the corner of the wood, follow the path to the left across the field to enter the wood and continue through it, heading uphill. Just before reaching the far edge, turn right at a crossroads of paths to head gently downhill; look out for a white arrow on a tree which points to the right. Cross a footbridge over a railway line, go down steps and walk along a path between trees and scrub, to emerge into a field. Keep ahead across the middle of the field, climb a stile, cross the busy A413 and climb a stile opposite to continue along the left-hand edge of a field, by trees on the left. Cross a footbridge over the River Misbourne and keep ahead to climb a stile in the field corner on to a road by Little Missenden church **F**.

The church is one of the oldest and most interesting in the Chilterns. It was founded in the late 10th century and there is Saxon, Norman and later work. The main features of interest are the murals, especially the 10ft-high (3m) one of St Christopher which was discovered in the 1930s. The village itself has a sleepy and secluded air, despite its proximity to the London–Aylesbury road, with a 17th-century manor house and some distinguished Georgian houses. Turn left through the village, re-crossing the River

The church at Little Missenden

Misbourne to rejoin the A413. Cross the road, take the slip-road opposite which bends right in front of a farm, and at a public footpath sign turn left over a stile **G**. On this next section the paths are narrow and likely to be overgrown in places. Climb another stile immediately ahead, continue along a path between wire fences, climb a stile and turn right. Turn left over a footbridge to re-cross the railway line and turn left again on the other side. Do not turn right over the first stile but continue parallel to the railway and turn right over the next stile. Walk along a path between wire fences to another stile, climb it, continue ahead through the attractive Bray's Wood and climb a stile on to a road.

Turn right along the road through the modern residential area of Hyde Heath to a T-junction. Turn right, and at public footpath and bridleway signs turn left **H** along a broad tarmac path across a common, continuing along a rough track past houses. Follow this track which bends to the right to keep along the right-hand edge of woodland, and just before reaching a metal gate, turn right along a hedge-lined path to enter White's Wood. Continue through the woodland, heading downhill, and on emerging from the trees keep along the right-hand edge of a field, by the edge of the wood on the right. In the field corner pass through a belt of trees and continue along a hedge-lined path to eventually reach a road to the right of a farm **J**.

Turn right along the road for 1 mile (1.6km) – there is a footpath – back to Chesham. On entering the town bear left along Church Street, cross the main road, keep ahead and turn left by the clock tower to walk along the pedestrianised High Street to the starting point. ●

West Wycombe, Hughenden and Bradenham

Start	West Wycombe
Distance	8½ miles (13.7km)
Approximate time	4½ hours
Parking	West Wycombe (garden centre)
Refreshments	Pubs and tearooms at West Wycombe, pub at Naphill, pub at Bradenham
Ordnance Survey maps	Landrangers 175 (Reading & Windsor) and 165 (Aylesbury & Leighton Buzzard), Explorer 3 (Chiltern Hills South)

Three National Trust properties are linked by this walk. Two of them, Hughenden Manor and Bradenham Manor, have connections with Benjamin Disraeli; the third, West Wycombe House, is associated with Sir Francis Dashwood and the notorious 'Hell-Fire Club'. Between the three are some splendid areas of beech woodland and fine open views, the latter especially on the final stage of the walk along a wooded ridge path. Waymarking is generally good, but be particularly careful following the route directions across the thickly-wooded and potentially confusing Naphill Common. This is quite an energetic walk with plenty of ups and downs, but nothing particularly steep or strenuous.

The main street of West Wycombe is lined with attractive 17th- and 18th-century brick and timber-framed houses. To the south of the village lies the house and park of the Dashwoods, to the north the church and Dashwood Mausoleum – all the work of the versatile and colourful Sir Francis Dashwood in the mid-18th century. He was something of an enigma; on the one hand a cultured man of the arts responsible for the rebuilding of West Wycombe House and the redesigning of the park; on the other hand, founder of the Hell-Fire Club, a group of high-spirited young aristocrats who are alleged to have indulged in drunkenness, orgies and devil-worship, in the caves at West Wycombe, at the golden ball on top of the church, or at nearby Medmenham Abbey.

Turn right out of the car park downhill towards the village and just before reaching the main road turn left along West Wycombe Hill Road. Walk uphill, passing the entrance to the Hell-Fire Caves, and just after a left-hand bend turn right through a kissing-gate **Ⓐ**, at a public footpath sign, and head downhill along the right-hand edge of a field, by a wire fence and line of trees on the right. Look out for a stile on the right, climb it, turn left and continue along the left-hand edge of a field to climb a stile on to a road.

Cross the road, climb a stile opposite and bear left diagonally across a field towards trees. Go through a gate, pass under a railway bridge, climb a stile and continue uphill along the left-hand edge of a field, by a wire fence on the left. Climb another stile and continue first through a narrow belt of trees and then along the left-hand edge of the next field. On the hill behind you there is a superb view of West Wycombe church and the Dashwood Mausoleum. Head downhill, climb a stile, cross a track, climb another stile and continue uphill along a broad grassy path towards a barn. Climb a stile, pass to the right of the barn and bear left along the lane ahead.

The lane leads gently downhill; at the bottom bear right, at a public footpath sign, on to a grassy path through an area of trees. Just before reaching a post with a white arrow and by a tree on the left with white arrows on it, turn right **B** on to an uphill path – there is another white arrow on a tree just in front to confirm that you are on the right route. Continue through woodland, and on emerging from the trees keep along the left-hand edge of a field, by a hedge on the left.

Go through a metal kissing-gate in the field corner, keep ahead to pass between cottages, go through another metal kissing-gate and turn right to the road on the edge of Downley Common **C**.

Bear right, walk diagonally across the corner of the common – this part is a cricket field – and head downhill along the clear, grassy path ahead between bushes. Pass to the left of Emery's Dairy, then bear right on to a wider track and continue downhill. Just after passing to the left of the Methodist church you reach a footpath sign **D**; here turn sharp left (not half-left) on to a path that soon heads into trees. At a path junction bear right, in the direction of the blue waymark, and

continue along the valley bottom through glorious woodland. On emerging from the trees keep ahead across sloping fields along a path between wire fences to re-enter more woodland. The path winds gently uphill and, after leaving the trees once more, it continues along a tarmac drive, between walls, passing the entrance to Hughenden Manor on the right.

Hughenden was the home of Benjamin Disraeli, bought by the young and up-and-coming politician in 1847, but it was not until the 1860s that he could afford to have it enlarged and reconstructed as the present imposing mansion. Inside it is full of pictures and mementoes of the great statesman, and remains much as he left it

when he died in 1881. Nearby is the small church, mainly a Victorian rebuilding, in which Disraeli is buried.

Continue downhill and a lovely view opens up on the right of the Hughenden valley, with the church below. Just after passing a cattle-grid turn left **E** through a gate, at a public footpath sign, on to a path that winds uphill through trees. Keep ahead at a path junction, go through a gate and continue along the left-hand edge of a field, by a wire fence and the edge of woodland on the left, to a stile. Climb it, immediately go through a kissing-gate at a T-junction of paths and tracks, and turn right, at a National Trust sign for Naphill Farm. Continue along a track which eventually leads on to a road on the edge of Naphill **F**.

Bear left along the road through the mainly modern village, and after $^1/_2$ mile (800m) turn left along Downley Road **G**. Look out for a public footpath sign where you turn right along a path between houses, enclosed by hedges, to emerge on to Naphill Common. Keep straight ahead across grass to pick up a path opposite which heads into trees; initially this is not very clear but soon there is a path junction and blue-waymarked post. Keep ahead along the bridleway through the

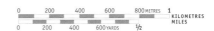

beautiful, thickly-wooded common, ignoring all side-paths, to reach another path junction by a field corner on the left. Bear right to head slightly downhill into a shallow hollow and then continue gently up to a T-junction of paths by a waymarked post.

Bear left along a track to continue through woodland, following blue waymarks and keeping more or less in a straight line, eventually joining a broad, stony track. Head downhill, take the right-hand track at a fork, continue down to a waymarked post and bear left between the edge of woodland on the left and a brick wall bordering the grounds of Bradenham Manor on the right. The track winds downhill to emerge on to the green at Bradenham. Most of this delightful village, with flint cottages and restored medieval church overlooking the large green, is owned by the National Trust. The 17th-century manor house, now a conference centre, was once the home of Disraeli's father.

Keep along the left side of the green, and at the bottom end turn right along a lane to a T-junction **H**. Turn left along a road and at the next T-junction turn right along the main road, in the direction of Aylesbury and Princes Risborough. After a short distance turn left through a metal

Hughenden Manor, home of Disraeli

kissing-gate, at a public footpath sign, and head across a field to climb a stile in the corner. Cross the railway line, climb another stile and continue to the edge of the trees to climb a half-hidden stile. Head uphill along the left-hand edge of a field to enter woodland, climb a stile and continue uphill through trees; in front of a farm turn left through a gate.

Follow the clear, straight track along a fine wooded ridge for $1\frac{1}{4}$ miles (2km) back to West Wycombe. Initially there are fine views to the left across to Bradenham village, church and manor, with the thick woodlands of Naphill Common beyond. Later, gaps in the trees reveal pleasant views over the valley to the right, and in front the golden ball on top of West Wycombe church tower is soon seen.

On reaching a parking area near the church, bear right **J** and head across the grass to pick up and follow a downhill grassy path that leads off from the far left-hand corner of the car park. The built-up area ahead is High Wycombe. The path passes to the left of West Wycombe church, almost completely rebuilt in the mid-18th century, and the impressive hexagonal Dashwood Mausoleum. Soon there is a superb view in front of the elegant façade of West Wycombe House.

At a fork take the right-hand path which continues down steps to reach the road opposite the starting point. ●

Chess Valley

Start	Stony Lane parking area between Little Chalfont and Latimer. Turn off A404 at Little Chalfont along lane signposted to Latimer and Flaunden, and parking area is ¼ mile (400m) along lane by left-hand bend
Distance	9½ miles (15.3km)
Approximate time	5 hours
Parking	Stony Lane parking area
Refreshments	Pub at Flaunden, pub at Commonwood, pubs at Sarratt, pub at Church End, pub at Chenies
Ordnance Survey maps	Landranger 165 (Aylesbury & Leighton Buzzard), Pathfinders 1139, TQ09/19 (Watford & Rickmansworth) and 1119, TL00/10 (St Albans & Hemel Hempstead)

The Chess is one of a number of small rivers that rise in the Chilterns and flow south-eastwards into the Thames Basin. This walk explores a particularly attractive part of the Chess valley, linking a series of villages – Latimer, Flaunden and Sarratt – lying to the north of the river, and one, Chenies, to the south. It is a varied route with some outstandingly beautiful woodland – especially along the southern edge of Chipperfield Common – grand views and pleasant, if sometimes muddy, walking across riverside meadows. It is also quite a hilly and energetic walk, though none of the climbs are particularly steep.

From the parking area turn left downhill along the road to a crossroads and keep ahead, in the Latimer and Flaunden direction, to cross the River Chess into Latimer, a small, pleasant village with an attractive green. Continue through the village and where the road curves slightly left, turn right **A** on to a path enclosed by wire fences which soon turns left and heads uphill to enter Long Wood.

At a fork take the left-hand path, continue through this attractive woodland and on reaching its right-hand edge, turn right to walk along a narrow, hedge-lined path, later continuing along a track to a T-junction of tracks. Turn left and follow a straight, broad, hedge-lined track into Flaunden; the track curves right to reach a road just to the right of the Victorian church **B**. Keep ahead to walk through the village and at a crossroads keep ahead again along a lane signposted to Belsize and Watford, which curves left to a T-junction **C**.

Climb the stile opposite, at a public footpath sign, and follow a path through the woodland of Lower Plantation, then continue along the left inside-edge of the wood to climb a stile on to a lane. Turn right along the lane for ¼ mile (400m) through Woodman's Wood and, where it bends right, keep ahead **D** over a stile, at

SCALE 1:26316 or about 2½ INCHES to 1 MILE 3.8CM to 1KM

| 0 | 200 | 400 | 600 | 800 METRES | 1 |
| 0 | 200 | 400 | 600 YARDS | | ½ |

KILOMETRES
MILES

a public footpath sign to Belsize, to continue along a path through the wood. Follow the main path all the while – there are some arrows on trees to help – and at a junction of several paths keep ahead by a line of posts on the right (the remains of

a former fence) to continue along the left inside-edge of the wood. After emerging from the trees keep along the left-hand edge of a field, by a hedge on the left, heading down to climb a stile on to a road at Belsize.

Turn left, take the first turning on the right and immediately turn right **E**, at a bridleway sign, on to a path that heads

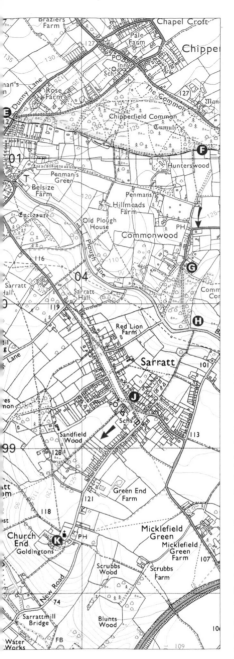

By the pond turn right **F** over a stile and walk along a path between a hedge on the left and a wire fence on the right. Climb a stile and continue between wire fences, bearing right to go through a metal kissing-gate at a corner of a lane. Keep ahead along the lane to the Cart and Horses at Commonwood, bear slightly right to continue along the lane, and at a fork take the left-hand lane **G** which descends through woodland to a T-junction. Turn left, then at a public footpath sign turn right **H** over a stile and walk along the left-hand edge of a field, by a wire fence on the left, heading up to climb a stile in the corner. Keep along the right-hand edge of the next field, by trees on the right, then bear slightly right to climb a stile and continue along a path enclosed by trees. At the end of the path turn right through a gap in the hedge, turn left along the left-hand edge of a field and continue along another enclosed path to a road. Keep ahead to a crossroads in Sarratt, a pleasant, spacious village with houses, cottages and two pubs grouped around a long green. The church, passed later on the walk, is ³/₄ mile (1.2km) away at Church End.

Turn right along The Green, passing the Cricketers and the village duck pond, and at a public footpath sign to Church End turn left **J** along a track. Climb a stile and continue along the left-hand edge of several fields, over a series of stiles, finally climbing two stiles in quick succession in a field corner to enter woodland. Continue through the trees, later keeping by a wire fence on the left, and head down to a track. Bear left, negotiate a metal kissing-gate and a stile, and follow a path along the left-hand edge of a field, by trees on the left. Where the trees end, bear slightly left and continue across the field – there is no visible path – making for the tower of Sarratt church just beyond the field corner. The church is mainly Norman,

uphill between trees and bushes. Cross a drive and continue along a wide level path that runs along the southern edge of the thickly wooded Chipperfield Common as far as Apostle's Pond, a small pool just to the left of the path where there is a bench. This is an exceptionally beautiful part of the walk and the route is well waymarked with blue arrows.

The River Chess near Chenies

enlarged over succeeding centuries, and nearby are a pub and some early 19th-century almshouses.

Do not climb the stile in the field corner but turn sharp right **K** in front of it to keep along the left-hand edge of the field, by a hedge on the left, to a stile. Climb it and ahead is a superb view over the Chess valley. Continue downhill along a tree-lined track, and at the bottom bear left across a field, making for a stile in the hedge on the far side.

Climb the stile and keep ahead, by a hedge and wire fence on the left, to go through a gate and descend steps on to a narrow lane. Turn left to Sarratt Bottom and at a T-junction turn right. Where the lane bends sharply right, turn left, at public footpath and Chess Valley Walk signs, through a metal gate **L**.

A quiet and pleasant section follows, through the Chess valley with the river to the left. Walk along a concrete drive and at the end of it bear slightly right to climb a stile. Continue across meadowland by the river, following Chess Valley Walk waymarks, climbing several stiles, passing through a small area of woodland and finally climbing a stile on to a lane. Bear left along the lane, cross the river and at a

fork bear left up to a road. Turn left and then go up steps **M**, pass through a wooden barrier and continue along a shady uphill path, parallel to the road, which curves right to go through another barrier to rejoin the road. Continue uphill into the village of Chenies, where church and manor house stand side-by-side in traditional fashion. The red-brick Tudor manor house belonged to the Russell family, dukes of Bedford, and inside the restored, mainly 15th-century church are several impressive Russell family monuments. Among those buried here is the Victorian Prime Minister, Lord John Russell.

Keep along the right-hand side of the triangular green and where the road bends left by a school, keep ahead, at a public bridleway sign, along a broad track. At a T-junction turn right and, opposite a concrete track on the right leading to Chenies Manor, turn left through a metal gate along a broad, tree-lined track. Go through another metal gate and follow an attractive path which runs along the side of the Chess valley, between scrub and bushes on the left and a wire fence on the right, with superb views to the right over the valley and Latimer village. The path enters woodland and emerges on to the road opposite the parking area. ●

Lardon Chase, Moulsford and Streatley

Lardon Chase, Moulsford and Streatley

Start	National Trust car park at Lardon Chase. On B4009, ½ mile (800m) west of Streatley opposite National Trust sign 'The Holies'
Distance	10 miles (16.1km)
Approximate time	5 hours
Parking	Lardon Chase
Refreshments	Pub at Moulsford, pub at Streatley
Ordnance Survey maps	Landranger 174 (Newbury & Wantage), Pathfinder 1155, SU48/58 (Wantage (East) & Didcot (South)), Explorer 3 (Chiltern Hills South)

A bracing start to this walk across the sweeping, empty expanses of the Berkshire Downs is followed by a descent into the Thames Valley. Then there is a delightful ramble along a lovely 2-mile (3.2km) stretch of the river between Moulsford and Streatley. At the end, a steep but short climb to the highest point on Lardon Chase – 453ft (138m) above the Goring Gap where the Thames cuts through between the Chilterns and Berkshire Downs – reveals magnificent views over the downs, Thames Valley and Chilterns. Although this is a long walk, much of it is across flat or gently undulating country and all the climbs are gradual, except for the final one.

At the car park walk back towards the road, but before reaching it turn sharp right, at a half-hidden public footpath sign, along an enclosed path which soon emerges on to the edge of a golf-course. Continue downhill in a straight line across the course, following the regular footpath signs. Near the bottom end, bear slightly left to head across to a public footpath sign by a metal gate. Go through the gate and walk along a tarmac track, passing to the right of barns, to a lane **A**, here joining the Ridgeway.

Turn left along the lane, which is tree-lined for most of the way, through the bottom of the valley for 1 mile (1.6km). At the entrance to Warren Farm, bear right at a Ridgeway sign to continue along a broad track for another 1¾ miles (2.8km). The track ascends gently and is tree- and hedge-lined, then it emerges into open country, with grand views over the Berkshire Downs. Soon after it starts to descend there is a crossroads of tracks **B**. Although the footpath sign is just in front, bear right here, in the 'Byway' direction, leaving the Ridgeway to continue along the track over the downs.

After ¾ mile (1.2km), at a crossroads of tracks where the arrow on a blue-waymarked post points to the left, turn right **C** on to the right-hand one of two

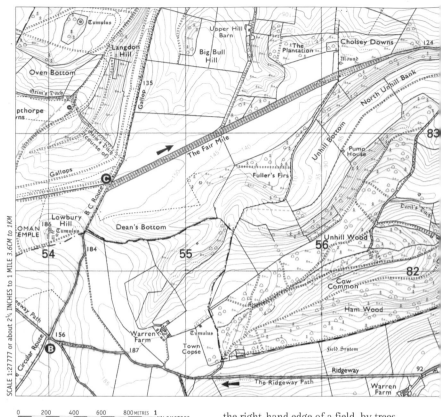

SCALE 1:27777 or about 2½ INCHES to 1 MILE 3.6CM to 1KM

0 200 400 600 800 METRES **1**
0 200 400 600 YARDS ½ KILOMETRES
MILES

straight, broad, parallel, grassy tracks and follow it for 2 miles (3.2km) across the downs. This is the 'Fair Mile', traditionally used for gallops, from which there are some superb views, especially across the valley to the right to the wooded ridge of Unhill Wood. Eventually the two tracks converge and the route continues along a single hedge-lined track to a road **D**.

Turn right to head downhill – it is a busy road but there is a grass verge. Where the road curves slightly to the right, turn left **E**, at a public footpath sign, on to a path that heads uphill across a field, continuing along the right-hand edge of a narrow, wooded embankment. At the end of the trees follow the path to the left, soon bearing right to head down to a yellow waymark. Here turn left between wooden fences, keep ahead through bushes and then turn right along the right-hand edge of a field, by trees and bushes on the right. In the field corner turn right through a gap in the trees to emerge on to the edge of a recreation ground. Do not continue across it but turn right along a path, between trees on the left and a wire fence on the right, to a road. Turn left and where the road ends, keep ahead along a path – later a track – to the main road at Moulsford **F**.

Turn right, take the first turn on the left, Ferry Lane, and follow it down between the buildings of the Beetle and Wedge Hotel to the riverbank **G**. Turn right through a kissing-gate to follow the riverside path for 2 miles (3.2km) to Streatley. This is a delightful stretch of the Thames, sometimes bordering woodland but mostly across open meadows, and passing Cleeve Lock; towards Streatley there is a particularly impressive view of the Goring Gap. Just after going through a gate into the final meadow, turn right to cross a footbridge on the edge of the

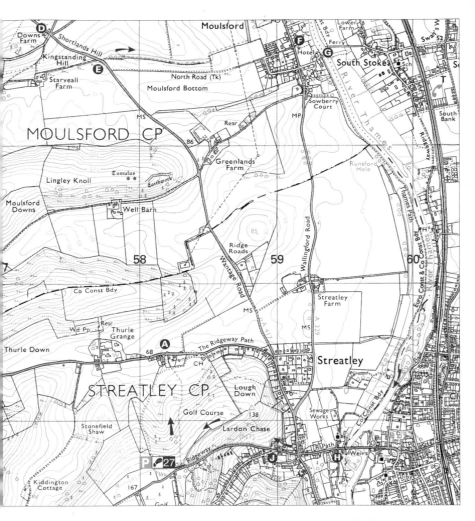

meadow and continue along a path to a gate. Go through it and walk along a shady tree-lined path which turns left and continues along a raised causeway into Streatley, passing to the left of the medieval church. Turn first right and then left by the church to reach a road **H**. Streatley lies on the western (Berkshire) bank of the Thames where the river cuts through the Goring Gap. There are some fine Georgian houses on the road leading down to the bridge, which links the village with its larger neighbour Goring on the opposite (Oxfordshire) bank.

Turn right through the village up to a crossroads and keep ahead, in the direction of Newbury. From here either continue along the road to return to the start or, for a more scenic finale, turn right **J** after 200 yds (183m) past the Old Schoolhouse along an uphill track. At a National Trust Lardon Chase sign, go through a gate and bear slightly left to follow a path steeply uphill across the open grassland to a stile and triangulation pillar at the top. From here there is a magnificent view over the Berkshire Downs, Thames Valley and Chilterns, with both Streatley and Goring churches below in the foreground on either side of the Goring Gap.

Do not climb the stile at the top but instead turn left in front of it, keep by the edge of trees on the right across the top of the chase and go through a gate to return to the car park. ●

Princes Risborough and Chinnor Hill

Start	Princes Risborough
Distance	10½ miles (16.7km)
Approximate time	5½ hours
Parking	The Mount car park, Princes Risborough
Refreshments	Pubs and cafés at Princes Risborough, pub at Bledlow
Ordnance Survey maps	Landranger 165 (Aylesbury & Leighton Buzzard), Explorers 2 (Chiltern Hills North) and 3 (Chiltern Hills South)

There is a definite feeling of remoteness on this peaceful, lengthy, hilly, but not particularly strenuous walk across a classic Chilterns landscape of rolling hills, beech woods and dry valleys. The route passes through three small villages, two of them little more than hamlets, all with interesting medieval churches, and there are superb views throughout. Undoubtedly the scenic highlight is the extensive vista across the Vale of Aylesbury from the Chiltern escarpment at the top of Chinnor Hill that comes suddenly and almost unexpectedly after emerging from woodland.

Despite recent suburban expansion, Princes Risborough preserves the air of a small traditional market town with an attractive market hall in the centre and an imposing church with a prominent tower and spire, largely restored in the 19th century. Opposite the church is the 17th-century manor house, a National Trust property. The town lies below the Chiltern escarpment, surrounded by impressive scenery, and from many points the Whiteleaf Cross – cut from the chalk hillside to the east – can be seen.

Start in Market Square and, with your back to the church, turn right along High Street. Turn left at a T-junction and at the roundabout in front turn right along New Road, heading uphill. Just before the top of the hill turn right **A**, at Icknield Way and footpath signs, to join the Ridgeway

and follow a hedge-lined track which descends to the A4010 **B**.

Turn left along the road – there is a footpath – take the first turning on the right, Upper Icknield Way, and follow the lane over a crossroads. At a Ridgeway sign bear left **C** on to a path that heads across a field and go through a metal kissing-gate. Continue between hedges, cross a railway line, go through another gate and continue downhill across the next field, heading for the left-hand side of a line of trees. Go through a kissing-gate, walk along an enclosed path and cross another railway line. Climb a stile and continue along a path, between wire fences and with trees and hedges on the left, gently uphill across a golf course. The path curves right to a stile; turn left over the stile and keep straight ahead across the middle of a field, passing to the left of an isolated house and on to a lane **D**

Cross the lane and take the path opposite along the left-hand edge of a field, by a hedge on the left. Follow the curving field-edge, climbing gently, continue through a hedge-gap into the next field and about 50 yds (46m) ahead, just before the path starts to curve right, turn left through a wide gap in the hedge. Continue along a broad, straight, grassy path, with lovely views over a rolling Chilterns landscape, heading downhill. At the bottom, pass through a hedge-gap, keep ahead across a field, go through a metal gate and continue uphill, by a wire fence on the right, towards farm buildings.

Go through a metal gate to the left of the buildings and keep ahead to join a tarmac drive. Where the drive curves slightly right, turn left over a stile, at a public footpath sign, on to a narrow path, between a hedge on the left and garden fences on the right, and head downhill through an area of woodland to a stile. Climb it, continue downhill along the left-hand edge of a field, by a wire fence and woodland on the left, and then ascend slightly to climb two stiles in quick succession. Continue along the left-hand edge of a field, climb a stile on to a tarmac drive and turn right to reach a road **E**.

Turn right, and then just past an entrance to a house turn left over a stile, at a public footpath sign, and walk along the left-hand edge of a field, by trees on the left, heading downhill; the path curves left to a stile in the field corner. Climb the stile and almost immediately turn right to follow a narrow, indistinct and possibly overgrown path that winds through an area of scrub and then continues steeply downhill along the right-hand edge of a field and through an area of scattered trees to a stile. Climb it, keep ahead through scrub and then continue along the right-hand edge of a field. Where the field-edge bends right, keep straight

ahead, making for a stile in the hedge on the opposite side which leads on to a lane. Turn left downhill into Radnage, passing the church on the left. This delightful 13th-century building, noted for its wall paintings, stands in an isolated position on the hillside presiding over the hamlet, which is little more than a collection of scattered, widely spaced cottages.

Opposite the lane which leads to the church turn right **F** over a stile, at a public footpath sign, and head straight across a narrow field to climb another stile. Continue across grass to pass through a gap in a fence on to a lane. Turn right and where the lane bends left keep ahead, at a public bridleway sign, along a tree-lined tarmac track. Where the track bends right through a gate, continue along a shady hedge-lined path as far as a T-junction. Turn left and continue along a tree-lined path which enters Sunley Wood.

Immediately turn right – the junction of paths is indicated on a tree trunk – on to a narrow path which heads uphill through the wood to a road. Turn left along it for nearly $^1/_2$ mile (800m), and just before a left-hand bend turn right **G** along Hill Top Lane. Continue through woodland, passing detached houses and a row of cottages, to a parking area. At the end of this parking area follow the track to the left and then turn right, at a blue-waymarked post, to enter Chinnor Hill Nature Reserve. Continue along a straight path through attractive woodland, and on emerging from the trees a short detour to the left brings you to the magnificent viewpoint on Chinnor Hill, looking over the Vale of Aylesbury from the edge of the Chiltern escarpment, with Chinnor village immediately below.

Keep ahead along the path which now heads downhill into woodland once more. At a fork follow the direction of the blue waymark to take the right-hand lower path and continue downhill to a junction of paths to the left of a house. Bear right

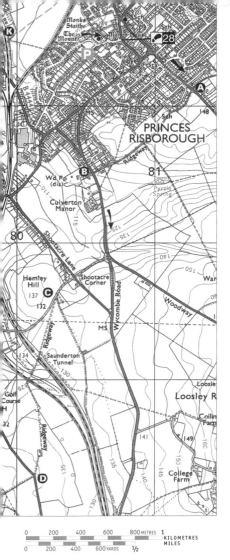

PRINCES
RISBOROUGH

| 0 | 200 | 400 | 600 | 800 METRES | 1 |
| 0 | 200 | 400 | 600 YARDS | ½ |

KILOMETRES
MILES

tarmac drive to go through a gate. Keep ahead past farm buildings, climb a stile and continue along the right-hand edge of a field, by a hedge and wire fence on the right, to climb another stile. Ahead, Whiteleaf Cross can be seen on the escarpment above Princes Risborough. Keep along the right-hand edge of the next field, climb a stile and turn left to follow a path through a narrow belt of trees. The path turns right into a field; keep along its left-hand edge, by a hedge on the left, and where the hedge finishes continue straight across the field to a stile. Climb it, keep ahead across the next field, later by a hedge and fence on the right, and climb another stile on to a lane in the hamlet of Horsenden.

Continue along the lane ahead, passing to the left of the tiny church; at one time it was bigger but the nave was pulled down in the 18th century, leaving just the chancel. Cross a stream, turn left through a gate **J** beside a thatched cottage, at a public footpath sign and climb a stile. Pass to the right of a barn, climb another stile and follow a path across a field. Continue along a track, go through a gate and follow a straight tarmac drive through the Princes Industrial Estate, passing under a railway bridge and keeping ahead to a road.

Cross the road and bear slightly left along a tarmac drive, passing houses, farm buildings and stables. Go under another railway bridge and then turn right **K**, at a public footpath sign, to follow a path across a field. The tower and spire of Princes Risborough church can be seen in front with Whiteleaf Cross beyond. At the far end of the field go through a metal kissing-gate, descend steps, cross a railway line, ascend steps on the other side and go through another kissing-gate. Walk along a path ahead to a road and continue along the road to a T-junction. Turn left and the road leads back via the church to Market Square. ●

and in front of the house bear left, go through a gate and continue along a downhill track. Where the track curves right, keep straight ahead across a field towards the white building ahead which is the Lion's Inn at Bledlow. Pass through a hedge-gap on the far side of the field, keep ahead past the inn and continue along the lane through this quiet and attractive village, passing to the right of the medieval church.

At a T-junction turn left and at the beginning of a row of houses turn right **H** along a track, at a public footpath sign. Climb a stile and continue along a

Further Information

 ### The National Trust

Anyone who likes visiting places of natural beauty and/or historic interest has cause to be grateful to the National Trust. Without it, many such places would probably have vanished by now.

It was in response to the pressures on the countryside posed by the relentless march of Victorian industrialisation that the trust was set up in 1895. Its founders, inspired by the common goals of protecting and conserving Britain's national heritage and widening public access to it, were Sir Robert Hunter, Octavia Hill and Canon Rawnsley: respectively a solicitor, a social reformer and a clergyman. The latter was particularly influential. As a canon of Carlisle Cathedral and vicar of Crosthwaite (near Keswick), he was concerned about threats to the Lake District and had already been active in protecting footpaths and promoting public access to open countryside. After the flooding of Thirlmere in 1879 to create a large reservoir, he became increasingly convinced that the only effective way to guarantee protection was outright ownership of land.

The purpose of the National Trust is to preserve areas of natural beauty and sites of historic interest by acquisition, holding them in trust for the nation and making them available for public access and enjoyment. Some of its properties have been acquired through purchase, but many have been donated. Nowadays it is not only one of the biggest landowners in the country, but also one of the most active conservation charities, protecting 581,113 acres (253,176 ha) of land, including 555 miles (892km) of coastline, and over 300 historic properties in England, Wales and Northern Ireland. (There is a separate National Trust for Scotland, which was set up in 1931.) Furthermore, once a piece of land has come under National Trust ownership, it is difficult for its status to be altered. As a result of parliamentary legislation in 1907, the Trust was given the right to declare its property inalienable, so ensuring that in any subsequent dispute it can appeal directly to parliament.

As it works towards its dual aims of conserving areas of attractive countryside and encouraging greater public access (not easy to reconcile in this age of mass tourism), the Trust provides an excellent service for walkers by creating new concessionary paths and waymarked trails, maintaining stiles and foot bridges and combating the ever-increasing problem of footpath erosion.

For details of membership, contact the National Trust at the address on page 95.

 ### Walkers and the Law

The average walker in a national park or other popular walking area, armed with the appropriate Ordnance Survey map, reinforced perhaps by a guidebook giving detailed walking instructions, is unlikely to run into legal difficulties, but it is useful to know something about the law relating to public rights of way. The right to walk over certain parts of the countryside has developed over a long period, and how such rights came into being is a complex subject, too lengthy to be discussed here. The following comments are intended simply as a helpful guide, backed up by the Countryside Access Charter, a concise summary of walkers' rights and obligations drawn up by the Countryside Commission.

Basically there are two main kinds of public rights of way: footpaths (for walkers only) and bridleways (for walkers, riders on horseback and pedal cyclists). Footpaths and bridleways are shown by broken green lines on Ordnance Survey Pathfinder and Outdoor Leisure maps and broken red lines on Landranger maps.

There is also a third category, called byways: chiefly broad tracks (green lanes) or farm roads, which walkers, riders and cyclists have to share, usually only occasionally, with motor vehicles. Many of these public paths have been in existence for hundreds of years and some even originated as prehistoric trackways and have been in constant use for well over 2000 years. Ways known as RUPPs (roads used as public paths) still appear on some maps. The legal definition of such byways is ambiguous and they are gradually being reclassified as footpaths, bridleways or byways.

The term 'right of way' means exactly what it says. It gives right of passage over what, in the vast majority of cases, is private land, and you are required to keep to the line of the path and not stray on to the land on either side. If you inadvertently wander off the right of way – either because of faulty map-reading or because the route is not clearly indicated on the ground – you are technically trespassing and the wisest course is to ask the nearest available person (farmer or fellow walker) to direct you back to the correct route. There are stories about unpleasant confrontations between walkers and farmers at times, but in general most farmers are co-operative when responding to a genuine and polite request for assistance in route-finding.

Obstructions can sometimes be a problem and probably the most common of these is where a path across a field has been ploughed up. It is legal for a farmer to plough up a path provided that he restores it within two weeks, barring exceptionally bad weather. This does not always happen and here the walker is presented with a dilemma: to follow the line of the path, even if this inevitably means treading on crops, or to walk around the edge of the field. The latter course of action often seems the best but this means that you would be trespassing and not keeping to the exact line of the path. In the case of other obstructions which may block a path (illegal fences and locked gates etc), common sense has to be used in order to negotiate them by the easiest method – detour or removal. You should only ever remove as much as is necessary to get through, and if you can easily go round the obstruction without causing any damage, then you should do so. If you have any problems negotiating rights of way, you should report the matter to the rights of way department of the relevant council, which will take action with the landowner concerned.

Apart from rights of way enshrined by law, there are a number of other paths available to walkers. Permissive or

FURTHER INFORMATION ● 91

concessionary paths have been created where a landowner has given permission for the public to use a particular route across his land. The main problem with these is that, as they have been granted as a concession, there is no legal right to use them and therefore they can be extinguished at any time. In practice, many of these concessionary routes have been established on land owned either by large public bodies such as the Forestry Commission, or by a private one, such as the National Trust, and as these mainly encourage walkers to use their paths, they are unlikely to be closed unless a change of ownership occurs.

Walkers also have free access to country parks (except where requested to keep away from certain areas for ecological reasons, eg. wildlife protection, woodland regeneration, safeguarding of rare plants etc), canal towpaths and most beaches. By custom, though not by right, you are generally free to walk across the open and uncultivated higher land of mountain, moorland and fell, but this varies from area to area and from one season to another – grouse moors, for example, will be out of bounds during the breeding and shooting seasons and some open areas are used as Ministry of Defence firing ranges, for which reason

access will be restricted. In some areas the situation has been clarified as a result of 'access agreements' between the landowners and either the county council or the national park authority, which clearly define when and where you can walk over such open country.

The Ramblers' Association

No organisation works more actively to protect and extend the rights and interests of walkers in the countryside than the Ramblers' Association. Its aims are clear: to foster a greater knowledge, love and care of the countryside; to assist in the protection and enhancement of public rights of way and areas of natural beauty; to work for greater public access to the countryside; and to encourage more people to take up rambling as a healthy, recreational leisure activity.

It was founded in 1935 when, following the setting up of a National Council of Ramblers' Federations in 1931, a number of federations earlier formed in London, Manchester, the Midlands and elsewhere came together to create a more effective pressure group, to deal with such problems as the disappearance and

Oxford's 'dreaming spires' from Old Boars Hill

Countryside Access Charter

Your rights of way are:

- public footpaths – on foot only. Sometimes waymarked in yellow
- bridle-ways – on foot, horseback and pedal cycle. Sometimes waymarked in blue
- byways (usually old roads), most 'roads used as public paths' and, of course, public roads – all traffic has the right of way

Use maps, signs and waymarks to check rights of way. Ordnance Survey Pathfinder and Landranger maps show most public rights of way

On rights of way you can:

- take a pram, pushchair or wheelchair if practicable
- take a dog (on a lead or under close control)
- take a short route round an illegal obstruction or remove it sufficiently to get past

You have a right to go for recreation to:

- public parks and open spaces – on foot
- most commons near older towns and cities – on foot and sometimes on horseback
- private land where the owner has a formal agreement with the local authority

In addition you can use the following by local or established custom or consent, but ask for advice if you are unsure:

- many areas of open country, such as moorland, fell and coastal areas, especially those in the care of the National Trust, and some commons
- some woods and forests, especially those owned by the Forestry Commission
- country parks and picnic sites
- most beaches
- canal towpaths
- some private paths and tracks Consent sometimes extends to horse-riding and cycling

For your information:

- county councils and London boroughs maintain and record rights of way, and register commons
- obstructions, dangerous animals, harassment and misleading signs on rights of way are illegal and you should report them to the county council
- paths across fields can be ploughed, but must normally be reinstated within two weeks
- landowners can require you to leave land to which you have no right of access
- motor vehicles are normally permitted only on roads, byways and some 'roads used as public paths'

obstruction of footpaths, the prevention of access to open mountain and moorland and increasing hostility from landowners. This was the era of the mass trespasses, when there were sometimes violent confrontations between ramblers and gamekeepers, especially on the moorlands of the Peak District.

Since then the Ramblers' Association has played an influential role in preserving and developing the national footpath network, supporting the creation of national parks and encouraging the designation and waymarking of long-distance routes.

Our freedom to walk in the countryside is precarious and requires constant vigilance. As well as the perennial

problems of footpaths being illegally obstructed, disappearing through lack of use or extinguished by housing or road construction, new dangers can spring up at any time.

It is to meet such problems and dangers that the Ramblers' Association exists and represents the interests of all walkers. The address to write to for information on the Ramblers' Association and how to become a member is given on page 95.

Walking Safety

Although the reasonably gentle countryside that is the subject of this book offers no real dangers to walkers at any time of the year, it is still advisable to take sensible precautions and follow certain well-tried guidelines.

Always take with you both warm and waterproof clothing and sufficient food and drink. Wear suitable footwear, ie. strong walking boots or shoes that give a good grip over stony ground, on slippery slopes and in muddy conditions. Try to obtain a local weather forecast and bear it in mind before you start. Do not be afraid to abandon your proposed route and return to your starting point in the event of a sudden and unexpected deterioration in the weather.

All the walks described in this book will be safe to do, given due care and respect, even during the winter. Indeed, a crisp, fine winter day often provides perfect walking conditions, with firm ground underfoot and a clarity unique to this time of the year.

The most difficult hazard likely to be encountered is mud, especially when walking along woodland and field paths, farm tracks and bridleways – the latter in particular can often get churned up by

On the Dunstable Downs

cyclists and horses. In summer, an additional difficulty may be narrow and overgrown paths, particularly along the edges of cultivated fields. Neither should constitute a major problem provided that the appropriate footwear is worn.

 Useful Organisations

Chiltern Society
PO Box 1029, Marlow, Buckinghamshire SL7 2HZ

Council for the Protection of Rural England
Warwick House, 25 Buckingham Palace Road, London SW1W 0PP
Tel. 0171 976 6433

Countryside Commission
John Dower House, Crescent Place, Cheltenham, Gloucestershire GL50 3RA
Tel. 01242 521381

Forestry Commission
Information Department, 231 Corstorphine Road, Edinburgh EH12 7AT
Tel. 0131 334 0303

Long Distance Walkers' Association
10, Temple Park Close, Leeds, West
Yorkshire LS15 0JJ
Tel. 0113 264 2205

National Trust
Membership and general enquiries:
PO Box 39, Bromley, Kent BR1 3XL
Tel. 0181 315 1111

Thames and Chilterns Regional Office:
Hughenden Manor, High Wycombe,
Buckinghamshire HP14 4LA
Tel: 01494 528051

Ordnance Survey
Romsey Road, Maybush, Southampton
SO16 4GU
Tel. 0345 330011 (Lo-call)

Ramblers' Association
1/5 Wandsworth Road, London SW8 2XX
Tel. 0171 582 6878

Tourist Information
Southern Tourist Board
40 Chamberlayne Road, Eastleigh,
Hampshire SO5 5JH
Tel. 01703 620006

Local tourist information offices:
Abingdon: 01235 522711
Amersham: 01494 729492
Aylesbury: 01296 330559
Dunstable: 01582 471290
High Wycombe: 01494 421892
Luton: 01582 401579
Maidenhead: 01628 781110
Newbury: 01635 519562
Oxford: 01865 726871
Reading: 01734 566226
Richmond: 01748 850252
Thame: 01844 212834
Wallingford: 01491 826972
Wantage: 01235 760176
Wendover: 01296 696759
Windsor: 01753 852010

Youth Hostels Association
Trevelyan House, 8 St Stephen's Hill, St
Albans, Hertfordshire AL1 2DY
Tel. 01727 855215

 **Ordnance Survey Maps
of the Chilterns and the
Thames Valley**

The Chilterns and Thames Valley area is
covered by Ordnance Survey 1:50 000
scale (2cm to 1km or 1 $\frac{1}{4}$ inches to 1 mile)
Landranger map sheets 164, 165, 166,
174, 175, 176 and 177. These all-purpose
maps are packed with information to help
you explore the area. Viewpoints, picnic
sites, places of interest, caravan and
camping sites are shown, as well as
information on public rights of way such
as footpaths and bridleways.

To examine the area in more detail, and
especially if you are planning walks,
Ordnance Survey Explorer Maps 2
(Chiltern Hills North) and 3 (Chiltern Hills
South), both at 1:25 000 scale (4cm to
1km or 2 $\frac{1}{2}$ inches to 1 mile) are ideal. The
following Pathfinder maps at 1:25 000
scale also cover the area:

1069 (SP 42/52)	1136 (SU 49/59)
1070 (SP 62/72)	1139 (TQ 09/19)
1071 (SP 82/92)	1140 (TQ 29/39)
1072 (TL 02/12)	1141 (TQ 49/59)
1073 (TL 22/32)	1155 (SU 48/58)
1074 (TL 42/52)	1158 (TQ 08/18)
1092 (SP 41/51)	1159 (TQ 28/38)
1093 (SP 60/61)	1160 (TQ 48/58)
1095 (TL 01/11)	1171 (SU 47/57)
1096 (TL 21/31)	1172 (SU 67/77)
1097 (TL 41/51)	1173 (SU 87/97)
1116 (SP 40/50)	1174 (TQ 07/17)
1119 (TL 00/10)	1175 (TQ 27/37)
1120 (TL 20/30)	1176 (TQ 47/57)
1121 (TL 40/50)	

To get to the Chilterns and the Thames
Valley, use the Ordnance Survey Great
Britain Routeplanner Travelmaster map
number 1 at 1:625 000 scale (1cm to
6.25km or 1 inch to 10 miles) or
Travelmaster map 6 (East Midlands & East
Anglia including London) and
Travelmaster 9 (South East England
including London) both at 1:250 000 scale
(1cm to 2.5km or 1 inch to 4 miles).

Ordnance Survey maps and guides are
available from most booksellers, stationers
and newsagents.

Further Information

Index

Abingdon 10, 29
Aldbury 11, 62, 64
Amersham 10, 38
Ashridge 62
  Park 64
Asquith, Herbert 8, 31
Aston 50
  Hill 32
  Woods 33
Attlee, Clement 8

Beacon Hill 69
Beaconsfield 14
Belsize 80
Berkhamsted 10, 11, 56
  Castle *58*
Berkshire Downs 8, 9, 20, 21, 36, 37, 83, 85
Bisham *61*
  Woods 42
Bledlow *10*, 11
Blyth, Edmund 35
Boer War, the 8
Boulter's Lock 24, 25
Bradenham 11, 75, 78
Bridgewater Monument 64
Bucklandwharf *32*
Burnham Beeches 14, *15*

Chalfont St Giles 38, 39
Charles I 46, 47
Charles II 55
Chenies 8, 82
Chequers 8, 68
Chesham 71, 74
Chess
  Valley 79
  River 9, 82
Chiltern Society 11, 94
Chilterns 8, 9, 11, 20, 23, 31, 35, 36, 43, 44, 50, 56, 65, 71, 79, 83, 85, 86, 87
Chinnor Hill 8, 86
  Nature Reserve 87
Chipperfield Common 79, 81
Christmas Common 16, 17
Churchill, Winston 70
Cliveden 24, 25
Cock Marsh 41
Cockshoots Wood 44
Commonwealth Air Forces Memorial 53
Cookham 25, 41
  Moor 43

Coombe Hill 8, 64, 68, 70
Cooper's Hill 9, 53, 54
Cuckhamsley Hill *18*
Culham 29
Cumnor 20

Dashwood, Sir Francis 75
Didcot 29
Disraeli, Benjamin 8, 76, 77
Dorchester 22
  Abbey 23
Drayton Beauchamp 32
Dunstable Downs 8, 34, 64, *94*
Dyke Hills 22, 23

Edward VIII 49
Egypt Woods *15*
Elizabeth I 10, 47
Ellesborough 69
Eton 10, 26, 27
Eton Wick 28
Evans, Sir Arthur 20

'Fair Mile', the 84
Fingest 11, 65

George II 49
George III 53, 55
Goring 85
  Lock *9*
Grand Union Canal 11, *32*, 58
Great Hampden 44, *46*

Hambleden 8, 11, 50, *52*
Hampden, John 46
Hampton Court Palace 10
'Happy Valley' 59, 60
'Hell-Fire Club', the 75
Henley-on-Thames 50, 52
Henry VII 10, 47
Herberts Hole 72
High Wycombe 10
Horsenden 89
Hughenden 75
  Manor 8, *78*
Hurley 10, 59

Ibstone 65
Icknield Way 9, 86
Ivinghoe Beacon 8, 62, *64*, 68

Jarn Mound 20
John, King 10

Kennedy, John F. 53
Kensworth Quarry 34

Lardon Chase 83
Latimer 79, 82
Little Hampden 44
Little Missenden 71, 74
London 9
Long Walk 53
Long Wood 79
Lower Plantation 79

Macmillan, Harold 27
Magna Carta, signing of 53
Maple Wood 70
Marlow 10, 43, 59
Medmenham Abbey 75
Milton, John 38, 40
Misbourne, River 9, 38, 74
Moulsford 83, 84

Naphill Common 75, 78
National Trust 8, 24, 34, 56, 62, 64, 68, 75, 86, 90, 95
Northchurch 56, 57

Old Boars Hill 20, *92*
Old Elvendon Wood 37
Orwell, George 8, 31
Oxford 20, *92*, 8, 16
Oxford Preservation Trust 20, 21
Oxfordshire Way 17

Pembroke Lodge 48
Penley Wood 67
Petersham 47
Pitstone Hill 62
Pitt, William (the Elder) 27
Prestwood 8
Princes Risborough 10, 86, 89
Pyrton Hill 17

Remenham 52
  Wood 50
Richmond 9, 11, 49, 10, 11, 47, 48, *49*
Ridge Wood 50
Ridgeway 9, 11, 13, 16, 17, 19, 83, 86
Robertson Corner 34

Rodger's Wood 38
Romney Lock 27
Round Hill 23
Royalty and Empi[re] Exhibition 27
Runnymede 10
Russell, Lord Joh[n] 82

Sarratt 11, 79, 81
Scutchamer Knob 1[8]
Sinodun Hills 23
Slough 14
Smith, W.H. 8, 52
Snow Hill 55
Spankers Hill Wood 48
Spencer, Stanley 25, 41, 43
Strand Water 25
Streatley 83, 85
Sutton Courtenay 8, *29*, 30

Temple Lock 59, 60
Thames 8, *9*, 12, 13, *28*, 30, 31, 36, *49*, 50, 51, 52, 55, 59
  Path 11
  Valley 11, 19, 20, 22, 23, 37, 41, 42, 48, 59, 83, 85
'Tree Cathedral' 34, 35
Turner, Joseph Mallord William 11
Turville 11, 65, *67*

Unhill Wood 84

Vale of Aylesbury 8, 35, 64, 68, *70*, 86, 87

Wallingford 10, *12*, 13
Watlington Hill 8, 16, *17*
Wendover 70
West Wycombe 75
Whipsnade 34
Whiteleaf Cross 86, 89
Whorley Wood 69
Widbrook Common 24, *91*
William the Conqueror 12, 26
Windsor 26
  Castle 10, *28*, 53, 55
Winter Hill 9, 41, *42*
Wittenham Clumps 9, 22, 23, 31
Wootton 20, 21
Wren, Sir Christopher 27, 52

Entries in italics refer to illustrations